The Root of all Money

What money is, how it gets its power, and how we let that power abuse us

COPYRIGHTS

THANK YOU

Thanks to the many people who have graced me with experience and insight on money matters throughout the years. Special thanks to Victor Grafe, David Murphy, Chris Shen, Jason and Hannah Gates, Lynda Grafe, Allen Shook, and all the others who reviewed and discussed these topics with me and helped refine the presentation; I only hope that the final version includes enough of your many good ideas. Even more special thanks to Elise Grafe, who combined insight into the concepts and artistic talent to bring key points to life in her illustrations. Thanks are also due to everyone who reads this and builds on a more thorough understanding of money to help us build and protect a better society.

TABLE OF CONTENTS

BIG THINGS AND LITTLE THINGS

Money. It's a big thing. A really big thing. It touches almost every aspect of our lives in some way. It enables us to reach our biggest goals. It prevents us from reaching our biggest goals. People with lots of it have lots of power. I am convinced that proper understanding of this big thing can help you master it. It will still be a big thing, but it will not be bigger than you. But how do you master such a big thing? By understanding it well enough to explain it simply. As Albert Einstein said, *If you can't explain it simply, you don't understand it well enough.*

I have always liked solving puzzles, and figuring out how things work. I have had the opportunity to get three university degrees (B.S. in electrical engineering, M.S. in electrical and computer engineering, and J.D. in law), graduating at the top of my class in each one. Seeking new puzzles to solve, new things to understand, I have worked with parallel computer architecture and robotics as a senior member of the technical staff at a national laboratory. I have earned national level soccer coaching licenses from two countries. I have filed hundreds of patent applications, been president of a technology startup, and helped found or finance almost two hundred new companies. In all the puzzles I've worked on, in every area from science to law to finance to management, I've found one principle to be universally true:

Big Things Are Made Of Little Things.

Understanding a big thing like money means that we have to understand the little things that it is made of.

Once you understand the little things, then you can master the big thing. But your understanding of the little things must be thorough enough that your explanations are simple. Big things have a way of trying to look complex, over and over again, so you need to have simple explanations that you can use to blow away the smoke, or pull back the curtain, and see the little things clearly when the big thing tries to overwhelm you.

We want to understand money well enough that we can explain it simply, especially to ourselves when it starts to look like money overwhelms our lives.

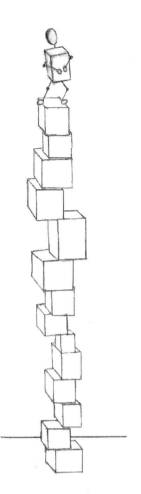

A MONEY MYSTERY

A few years ago, I had the opportunity to spend a few weeks in Kenya. I had heard many stories about the crazy traffic in Kenya: roads of decidedly uneven maintenance, home made speed bumps at odd intervals, cars going whichever way appeared to offer momentary advantage, total gridlock. I was told that to drive in Kenya (which I fortunately did not), all you had to do was get in the car and make up your mind that no one was going to intimidate you. In one traffic jam, I actually saw cars playing chicken with a steamroller as they tried to cut across freshly laid asphalt!

All that was going to change, I was told, with the new road that was being built in Nairobi. The road would be many lanes wide, and have modern entrance and exit ramps. It would go through the main parts of town, and eventually join up with a loop road around town. I saw parts of it under construction, and rode on the 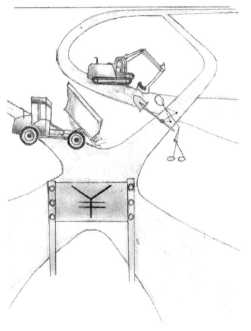 parts that were completed. It was an engineering and public works project that outshone most other Kenyan projects. This new road would solve many problems that had long plagued

Nairobi. I asked what made this important project finally possible. I was told the key step was getting funding from China.

I shared the excitement, since anything that could sort out the traffic would be a great advance. I observed the construction every time we drove on or by the new road: heavy machinery operated by local workers, and brigades of shovel-wielding laborers, big trucks full of asphalt, concrete, and steel. I am always curious about how people organize themselves to get things done, so I inquired about all of these. The cement and other materials came from plants in Kenya. The skilled workers were graduates of Kenya's vocational training schools. The unskilled laborers were available in plenty from the continual influx of people from rural areas to Nairobi looking for work.

As I considered all this, I could not escape one question: If Kenyan workers are using materials produced in Kenya to build a road on Kenyan land, for Kenyans to drive on, then *why did they need money from the Chinese*?

Our host had no real answer. Do you?

IS MONEY THE MASTER?

It's been said that money makes the world go around. We complain about too much money in politics. People bemoan having too much month at the end of the money. Magazines make lists of people with more money than everyone else. It seems like everything has a price tag, and you can't do anything without money. The rich get richer, and the poor get poorer, and protesters march and chant in opposition. In "It's a Wonderful Life," everyone was afraid of the power of Mr. Potter, the richest man in town. People with money seem to be able to do anything. These little pieces of metal and paper have so much power. Where do they get it?

Money has power over us only to the extent that we give it power. Money is an immensely powerful tool, but it is, at its core, only a tool. Money only exists in the context of a free, cooperative society, but we've let money reduce our freedoms and undermine our cooperation. Money exists only as our servant, but we act like that's not true. We bow down before a god that we created, before a god that exists only as long as we treat it as a god. The goal of this book is to examine the most fundamental foundations of money, to expose the root of all money, and give you the knowledge and perspective to let money serve you, instead of you serving money.

We'll look at the essentials of money, and how it came to be. We'll see what a great advantage it is to have money in a society. We'll also see how those who understand the mysteries of money can exploit it to gain power over those who do not. We'll also examine some of the common complaints around money, and better understand where to focus our efforts if we want to do anything about them.

If you can't explain it simply, you don't understand it well enough. We are going to start at the simplest possible explanations of money, to be sure we understand it well.

FOUNDATIONS OF MONEY

Q: Poor people have it. Rich people need it. If you eat only it you will die. What is it?

A: Nothing

Q. Rich people have it. Poor people need it. If you eat only it you will die. What is it?

A. Money

Money is everywhere, but there never seems to be enough in your pocket. Everyone wants more money. Just a little more money will make you happy. If you just give your bank account information to the friendly guy who asked by email for your help in swindling his third world country, you will get lots of money. Groucho Marx told us "While money can't buy happiness, it certainly lets you choose your own form of misery."

We spend a lot of our lives talking about and chasing after money, but do we really know what money is? The first step in exposing the root of money is to answer the question of "what is money?"

WHAT IS MONEY?

What do you think of when you hear the word "money"? Pieces of metal or paper you carry around? A bank statement showing a high balance? A credit card statement showing a low balance? Bits of information in electronic storage somewhere? Diamond necklaces and gold teeth? Before we can understand how money works, we have to understand what money is.

Dictionaries give various definitions. Money is defined as any of:

1. any circulating medium of exchange, including coins, paper money, and demand deposits;

2. paper money;

3. gold, silver, or other metal in pieces of convenient form stamped by public authority and issued as a medium of exchange and measure of value;

4. any article or substance used as a medium of exchange, measure of wealth, or means of payment, as checks on demand deposit or cowrie;

5. a particular form or denomination of currency.

Well, that tells us what money might look like, and maybe helps us recognize it when we see it. But it doesn't tell us what money truly is, the foundation of money. Maybe some examples will help. We are all familiar with coins and paper bills, issued by some government. It can be the local government, but it doesn't have to be – US dollars can be spent directly in most countries in the world. It doesn't even have to be physical coins and bills - credit cards and debit cards deal in dollars and cents without any actual bills and coins changing hands. There are other kinds of money, though.

In the copper mining region of what used to be Zaire, Africa, crosses made of copper were used as money. They ranged from about 0.5 to 2.5 pounds. If you were rich, you'd also have to be strong to carry your money.

In west Africa, kissi money was used: twisted iron bars with a T at one end and a spatula at the other. The length varied from 9 to 15 inches, depending on the value. Hard to carry in your wallet, and making change would be a challenge.

Canadian Tire money is a promotional coupon program issued by Canadian Tire, which started in 1958. Tire money is given out as bonuses when purchases are made and can be redeemed at face value at any Canadian Tire store or gas station, including the amount for taxes. Some merchants besides Canadian Tire accept tire money, because after all, merchants buy gasoline, too.

These look a little like "coins and bills" money, though in unusual (to us) forms. But consider rai stones, once used as

money on the island of Yap in Micronesia.
Large round stones, with a hole in the middle,
were quarried from nearby Palau Island. The
value of each stone depended on its size and
weight plus the difficulty in transporting them.

Value was also affected by the history of a particular stone, such
as how many people died transporting it. They were placed in
public places, and although ownership of a stone could change,
the location rarely did.

It's plain to see that money can take lots of forms, but that
doesn't tell us what money truly **is**. It doesn't have to be bills, or
coins, or iron bars, or copper crosses, or even big stones. With
this range of forms, it doesn't look like the form is essential to
what money is.

Maybe money is really just a way to store value or wealth.
You work, and you earn money, and so that money stores the
value of your work. This is a pretty common view, and for daily
decisions is probably a pretty useful one. However, this misses
the foundation of money, since we've just shifted the discussion
from "what is money?" to "what is value that can be stored in
money?"

As an illustration, let's take a huge pile of paper marks from
the early days of the Weimar Republic in central Europe, shortly
before World War II. Those marks represent a lot of value. We
want to store all that value in a safe place, so put them all in a

vault for 20 years or so. The money in the vault has not degraded or changed, but what has happened to the value? The marks might have value during a toilet paper shortage, or as fire starting material, but otherwise they're pretty much worthless. What happened to the value that you stored so safely in the money in your vault?

Objection: the Weimar Republic mark lost its value due to government printing presses and inflation, so that's not a fair look. OK, buy a rai stone in Micronesia and ship it to New York City. Let's assume that we can get it there fast enough so there is no inflation. How much value is stored in the big, heavy rock? More importantly, how much of the stored value can we get out of the rock? Can we pay for a cab with a chip off a rai stone? There must be something else to money than just a store of value, since money can't always be used to store or transfer value.

Another objection: Weimar Republic marks were a fiat currency - only money because the government says its money. Real money can only be things like gold or silver. We'll talk more about gold and silver later, but for now consider that gold and silver have some intrinsic value, for adornment purposes and for industrial uses. Part of their value is due to that intrinsic value, just like corn or pork bellies or paper or any other commodity. Gold and silver have advantages over other commodities in commerce - they are relatively dense stores (high value for low volume and weight), they don't wear out or rot or corrode, and they are easy to carry around. However, trading for commodities with intrinsic value is barter, not money. The intrinsic value of gold or silver is not the same as their value as money, just as the intrinsic value of the paper in the marks of the Weimar Republic was not the same as its value as money. Gold and silver may also have some use as money in addition to their intrinsic value, but that is not because of any magic properties of the metal. Once you discount for the intrinsic value of the metal (or the paper in the Weimer Republic marks), there is still some value left in the gold or silver coins. The value that is more than the intrinsic value of the underlying material is money, and that is what we need to understand.

Before we uncover the root of money, we need to be sure that we carefully define a few terms. We will use "**money**" as the term for the value that is represented by a "**marker**" for money. Markers for money are usually in some kind of system, such as bills or coins of various denominations. Those bills or coins will be referred to as "**currency**." In other words, currency is a specific kind of marker that represents whatever it is that makes money valuable. Currency can be things like dollar bills, or coins, or rai stones. Money is the concept behind what those markers represent. Every modern economy must have the same principle of money, although they can use different currencies. Both money and currency will refer to the pure forms of them, meaning what is left after any significant tangible value is disregarded. If a piece of currency has tangible value, and it is traded for the value of its tangible value, then you have a barter transaction and not a monetary one. Transactions in money in our discussion will concern only the intangible concept of money.

Money and currency have lots of definitions, and there is some risk to reusing those terms here. As you read on, try to start with a fresh look at those concepts, and keep the ideas of money and currency separate. We'll work out money first, then see what happens when you represent money with currency.

Next, we have to establish some foundational understandings about the nature of money. These take the form of some absolute, though perhaps unconventional, statements about money, so that we can build our understanding on a firm foundation.

To keep in mind:
1. **Money and currency are different.**
2. **Currency is the system of markers that represent money, and almost any system can work as currency.**
3. **If a currency has intrinsic value (e.g., the paper or metal that forms the currency), then the money represented by the currency is the value that exceeds that intrinsic value.**

FOUNDATION #1. MONEY IS <u>ONLY</u> CONCERNED WITH PEOPLE.

Money is only concerned with people. It has no direct effect on anything else in the world. Money can only affect the world by affecting the actions of people.

It is easy to see that money is at least **partly** about people. We work to earn money, we hire people and pay them with money, so we are familiar with trading money for someone's time or effort. But is money **only** about people? Does it really have no effect on anything else? What about the things you buy with money?

Let's look at what you do with money (in these examples, with the currency that represents money). You can put it in a jar and bury it. That money is not really about anything except displacing a little bit of dirt in the ground.

You can use money to hire someone to do something for you. Paying someone to work for you is clearly about people, trading money for a person's time and energy. You can get money by working for someone else. This is also clearly about people - trading your time and energy for money.

But the most common use of money is to buy things you want. One apple has a certain price, so it's

tempting to think of the apple as equivalent to that amount of money. It seems like this money is about the things you buy, and not about people. But that's one of the first mistakes about money that we have to correct.

Take the people out of the picture, and what do you have? Take your dollar bills and walk up to an apple tree and wave them at the tree. Does the tree give you its apples? Or throw some coins at a sheep. How much wool will the sheep give you? Or maybe slide your credit card across the ground; how much water or oil or coal springs up?

Most of the universe is not responsive to money. Mathematical concepts don't change due to money – the ratio of the circumference of a circle to its diameter will be pi no matter what happens with money. You can't buy off a reduction in gravity, or speed up light – physical laws do not pay attention to money. You can't pay animals to behave – your dog will chew up your slippers no matter how much money you offer him. There are estimated to be about 10^{80} atoms in the universe; none of them respond to money. There are about one million species of insects in the world, about one quintillion insects in all; none of them respond to money. There are only a few thousand tigers in the world, but not a single one responds to money. The only thing, the only creature, the only being in the universe that responds to money is people.

That's interesting, but we've all used money to buy things. We've all thought about the price of things in dollars. If money only works on people, how do you use money to buy things?

Take a simple example. Adam has an apple, and you want it. What do you need the apple to do? Nothing, except continue being an apple and doing what apples normally do. What do you need Adam to do? Allow you to take the apple, without invoking his right of self-defense or calling the rest of society to help him defend himself (that is, calling on the government to punish you for stealing). How do you get him to do what you want? You offer him money.

This simple example, played out in the hugely complex web of interactions among people, builds our whole economy. You can buy apples at the store because money induced action from the cashiers, the shelf stockers, the truck drivers, the truck builders, the fuel companies, the road builders, the tree growers, the apple pickers, the box makers, the people who make clothes for all those other people, the people who make steel for the people who make trucks, and so on and so on.

Nothing in the world responds to money except people. Money is only concerned with people. As we'll see next, money is even more limited than just people – money is concerned only with the **promises** of people.

To keep in mind:

1. Money is only concerned with people.
2. Money has no direct effect on anything else in the world.
3. Money can only affect the world by affecting the actions of people.

FOUNDATION #2. MONEY SHIFTS PROMISES ACROSS TIME AND SPACE.

Money is only a store of people's promises, used to give and take people's promises across different times and places, and in a range of quantities.

This foundation seems a little more outlandish than the previous one. We were just talking about money being used to induce someone to do something, and now we've switched to something ephemeral like a store of people's promises. How do you store a promise? How many promises can fit in a nickel? Why do more promises fit in a $20 bill than a dime? We generally don't think about promises being stored in your coins or bills or online balances.

To make this clear, we'll start with the simplest commerce between people, and build our way up to money.

First, some simple barter. Adam has an apple; Paul has a peach. Paul offers Adam a trade, and Adam accepts. Commerce happens, with no money and no promises.

Adam trades his apple to Paul for Paul's peach. Adam gets the peach; Paul gets the apple. A direct trade, with no future obligations and no money.

Next time Paul has a hankering for an apple, though, he is out of peaches. Paul does have a pumpkin, though. It's a nice, big pumpkin, worth at least two apples. If Adam has two apples, and Paul is ready to eat two apples, then they can still make a deal with no money. What if Adam doesn't have two apples though? Or Paul is not really hungry enough to eat two apples today?

Paul wants two apples for his pumpkin, Adam wants a pumpkin from Paul, but Adam has only one apple. How can Adam get the pumpkin?

Paul and Adam can strike a deal - Paul will give Adam the pumpkin now, and Adam will give Paul one apple now, plus one more apple tomorrow. Smart guys, Paul and Adam: they've invented a way to stretch a pumpkin across time. Paul wants to be sure that Adam doesn't forget to give him the apple, though, so Paul makes Adam write it down: "I, Adam, will give Paul one apple tomorrow." Adam's note records his promise to Paul to do something for Paul in the future. It is not money yet, but it's a start.

Adam offers Paul one apple now, plus a promise that Adam will give Paul a second apple later. Paul accepts Adam's real apple plus a promise of a second apple later, and Adam gets the pumpkin.

Tomorrow comes, and Paul doesn't really feel like apples. But he thinks some cheese would be nice. So Paul goes to Chester the cheese man, but Paul has nothing left to trade, since he already gave his peach and his pumpkin to Adam. Chester is willing to take an apple in trade for cheese, but Paul doesn't have an apple. Paul could go find Adam, and ask him to produce the apple he promised, and then take the apple to Chester to trade for the cheese. That's a lot of walking around, and Paul wants cheese now. Paul could save a lot of walking if he could convince Chester to take the apple promise note Paul got from Adam. Chester can go and get the apple directly from Adam whenever

Chester wants his apple. If Chester accepts that deal, then the note is now a lot more like money: Paul has received real cheese from Chester for the apple promise from Adam, as represented by Adam's note. Adam's apple promise note has been used by itself to buy something else.

Paul wants some cheese, but all he has is the apple-promise he got from Adam. Chester might want an apple later, so he accepts Adam's apple-promise in exchange for his cheese. Paul gets the cheese, and Chester gets the right to call on Adam's apple-promise. Adam's apple-promise has been traded like it was a real apple.

This kind of transaction is called "negotiable instruments" in law. Negotiable instruments have the same foundation as money, but they are still not quite money. You know this if you've ever tried to buy something with a check drawn on a new account, or from an out of town bank, or tried to pay with a credit card that the store doesn't accept. If the person on the other side of the deal doesn't trust the promise you offer, then there is no deal. If Chester the cheese man doesn't trust Adam the apple grower, then Paul doesn't get any cheese when he offers Adam's promise note to Chester. Maybe Chester had a bad experience with Adam in the past, or doesn't like Adam's apples, or has never heard of Adam, or doesn't believe Adam really has any apples. Whatever the reason, if Chester doesn't trust the promise in Adam's note, Paul goes cheese-less. If the store doesn't trust your out of town bank, then you don't get to pay with your check.

While trading in negotiable instruments is much easier than trading in physical goods, it can still be quite inconvenient. Everyone carrying around bits of promises from lots of different people, kind of like trading cards. "I'll trade you two Adam-apple-promises and one Chester-cheese-promise for one Tom-Tshirt-promise." What do you do if you move to another town? What happens if Tom runs out of Tshirts? What if bugs kill all Adam's apple trees?

Trading promises, like Adam's apple-promise, is a lot easier than carrying around physical items. But how do you compare apple-promises and cheese-promises and pumpkin-promises and wash-your-socks promises?

What we need to make all this work is some universal unit of promise, one that averages or combines all the various promises that we would trust from the various people in our trading circles. It has to be one that everyone trusts. It also has to have some consistent, dependable translation to value, so that we can use it to translate two apples to one pumpkin on one day, and one apple to one piece of cheese on another day. If we can achieve such a universal unit of promise, then we have **real money**. The tangible thing that is used to represent the unit of promise is a marker that signifies the unit of promise; the marker is what we will call currency.

When each transaction is valued in universal promise units, then those units can be freely traded in other transactions. Everyone can use the same notes, and no one has to figure out how to directly convert pumpkin-promises into wash-your-socks promises.

Let's go back to your real world experience. When someone offers you currency for your services, why do you accept the currency? Not because of the quantity of currency – only history buffs would assign any value to 1 billion Weimer Republic marks. Not because of the intrinsic value of the currency - nobody really needs small pieces of paper already defaced with colored ink, or a really big rock, with a hole in the middle, parked downtown. You accept the currency because you trust that someone else will accept it from you. That's the necessary condition – if you don't have the trust, you don't accept the currency. That is also the sufficient condition – if you do have that trust, you do not need anything else.

If you have the trust in the promise, nothing else matters about the currency. The currency offered can be ugly, and you will still accept it if you have that trust. The currency offered can be beautiful, but you will not accept it unless you have that trust. The currency can be gold or silver, but you will not accept it as money unless you trust that others will accept it as money. You might accept gold or silver in trade because you want some shiny metal, but it is not money unless other people, with no desire to possess shiny metal for its own sake, will also accept it as money. The quantity of currency has no meaning except as it translates to the quantity of services you can get from someone else. You are willing to trade something with immediate value (your time, or your right to retain something you have already acquired) for nothing more than an otherwise worthless marker **only** because of your confidence that someone else will take the otherwise worthless marker in a later trade.

Money thus provides an intermediate step in the barter that is commerce, like a negotiable instrument but without the need for personal, individual trust at each step. Without money, deals only happen when both parties have the same value to trade, and have that value ready at the same time. With money, deals can have wildly different intrinsic value (a whole cow for a little piece of paper?) since the money represents the rest of the value. Different deals can have different values, too, since you can take a large amount of money from one deal and spread it over many smaller deals, or combine money from small deals into a larger deal. Also, money allows deals to be spread over arbitrary times. You can trade services today for apples next week, or a car next year, by using money to temporarily store the promises.

For this to work, though, the trust in the currency has to be universal across a sufficiently large group of people. Since the currency you receive in exchange for your services has no value on its own, you will only accept it if you are certain that the people you want to trade with will also accept it. Money, which has no value by itself, acquires value when enough people act as though it has value. You can't do that with mathematical concepts - pi will not equal 3.0 no matter how many people believe it. You can't do that with physics - gravity will not stop even if we all agree it will. You can't do that with nature – dogs will chew slippers even if everyone believes they will not. Money has no value to dogs, gravity, or pi; and would have no value to people except that other people agree it has value. If enough people agree that money has value, then it becomes true. God said "Let there be light" and therefore there is light. People say "Money has value" and therefore money has value. Money only has the value that the cooperative transactions of the people in the society give it.

Money is a hugely important tool for cooperative social interactions. Money allows us to order our lives with finer resolution, buying and selling however much we need at the moment. Money allows us to trade across the whole world, instead of just with the few people that we personally know well enough to trust. Money allows us to shift value in time and place with minimal hassle. Since it gets its value only from the value assigned to it by people, it can be small and portable, and doesn't get old or go bad. These qualities of money make it an enormous force for good in the world, as we'll prove next.

To keep in mind:
1. **Money is only a representation of people's promises.**
2. **Money becomes money when enough people in a community accept it as money, and that only happens when they trust that others in the community will accept it as money.**
3. **Without that trust, there is no money, regardless of the currency attempted.**
4. **With that trust, there is money, regardless of the currency used to represent the money.**

FOUNDATION #3. VOLUNTARY TRADES IN MONEY ALWAYS INCREASE WEALTH.

Based on the fundamentals of money so far, we can now start to appreciate another key foundation, one that is critical to recognize if we are to get to the root of money and gain mastery over it. Money involves strictly voluntary transactions, and each transaction involving money always increases the **individual wealth** of the two parties involved, and the **total wealth** of the society. That claim goes against a lot of teaching about the evil of money, but it follows directly from the foundations of money that we've already developed.

We have to be careful about our terms, though. This principle applies only to voluntary transactions. If someone is compelled or forced to take part in a transaction, then you don't have a trade. You have a robbery. Money might be part of a forced transaction ("Your money or your life!"), but such a transaction is fundamentally based on the force and not on the money. Any transaction that is based on the money must be voluntary on both sides. Each part voluntarily agreed to make the trade. Even voluntary transactions made under unusual pressures are still voluntary – hungry gold miners paid outrageous prices for eggs, but they still voluntarily decided to make the purchase.

First let's look at the effect of a voluntary trade on individual wealth. Does every transaction based on money increase the wealth of each of the parties? We've all made purchases that we regret; how did those deals increase our wealth?

Voluntary means both parties wanted the things they got more than the things they already had. So, **as measured by the parties themselves**, "voluntary" means that each party by definition increases its individual wealth in every voluntary trade. Each party wanted the thing it received more than the thing it gave up, so each party got more wealthy (we'll define "wealth" more precisely below).

A purely voluntary transaction – Adam trades his extra spoon for Paul's extra bowl. Each party is better off.

But what about pet rocks? Does spending $5 to buy a pet rock really increase the individual wealth of the new pet rock owner? Absolutely yes - if the purchase was voluntary, then at the moment of the trade the buyer had decided that a pet rock was more desirable than the $5. We have objective, irrefutable evidence of that: he voluntarily made the trade. Individual wealth can decline after a trade, for example when the buyer realizes that his pet rock is a natural at "sit" and "stay," but can't seem to learn to "fetch." That decline in wealth is a consequence of the buyer's changing desires, though, and not of the trade itself. The voluntary trade is itself proof of the wealth increase on each side: at the moment of the trade, each side must have wanted the new thing more than the old thing or the voluntary trade would not have been made.

But what about when someone makes a losing trade out of compassion for another, or some other reason unrelated to wealth? You might not really want to pay for a stale candy bar, but you want to help your nephew with his fundraiser. Or you gave money to a charity, and didn't get anything in return. What about those deals? Your personal wealth didn't increase enough to outweigh the money you gave up, and you knew it at the time of the trade, but you still made the trade.

The answer to this objection lies in a better understanding of the meaning of "wealth." In its most general sense, your wealth is the measure of the conformance of the world to the way you want it to be. We expend our time to rearrange the world to be more like we want it to be. We mow the lawn not because we want the tiny pieces of grass the mower makes, but because we want a tidy yard and some exercise, and the good opinion of our neighbors, more than we want whatever else we would do with the time it takes to do the mowing. We trade our time for money at work, and then trade that money for tickets to a movie, because we want the entertainment of the movie more than we want the time we spent earning the money to trade for it.

When you buy the candy bar from your nephew, in your estimation the world is more like you want it to be (hence you are more wealthy) if you have a stale candy bar and a happy nephew than if you keep your money and your disappointed nephew keeps the stale candy bar. When you give to a charity, in your estimation the world is more like you want it to be if the charity uses the money than if you keep the money. So, in every trade, the total change to the world as a result of the trade must be deemed an improvement by both parties or the trade is not voluntary. Each party must increase their individual wealth at the moment of the trade.

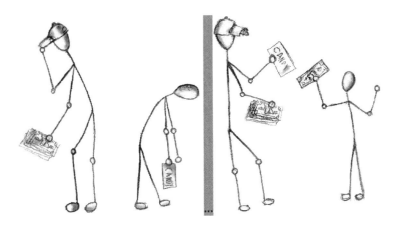

Do you want a world where you keep your money and your disappointed nephew keeps his fundraising candy bar?

Or a world where you have a stale candy bar, and your happy nephew has some of your money?

Wealth is more than just the money or things that change hands, and voluntary trades always increase wealth.

Another objection - what about when you buy something, but it doesn't turn out to be what you thought? Dr. So-and-so's snake oil doesn't really cure your baldness, or that exercise thingy doesn't really burn fat and build muscle effortlessly? How do those trades increase your personal wealth?

If you got what you wanted, but later changed your valuation of the thing, then it was your changing valuation that decreased your wealth. If you buy a dozen apples, and then decide that you like peaches better, it is your changing preference that decreased your wealth, not the trade. On a positive note, if you buy a dozen apples, and then decide that you like them a lot more than you thought, your changing valuation has increased your wealth.

If you got what you wanted at the time of the trade, but later events change its value to you, then it is those changing events that decrease your wealth. Maybe the snake oil worked when fresh, but its potency has been lost since you didn't try it until 10 years later when you started losing your hair. Or the apples you bought are not so tasty after sitting in your car for a week. The trade didn't decrease your wealth; the change of the item over time has decreased your wealth.

Sometimes, though, we get fooled - we really believed in the snake oil or the exercise thingy, but it wasn't really what they said it was. The thing we got, at the time of the trade, was not what we thought it was when we considered its value. It wasn't time, or our changing preferences, that did us in; it was the failure of the thing to be what we thought it was. In this scenario, you didn't really have a voluntary trade. You asked for an apple in trade for your chicken, but Adam gave you a cleverly painted rock, and you don't appreciate Adam's art as much as you appreciate apples. The exercise thingy might be a more subtle fraud, but it's the same principle. If you agree to a trade, and the other side doesn't give you what you agreed, then there was no voluntary trade. This is theft with more subtlety and sophistication, but it's still theft. We call that theft "fraud" and give a claim for damages to the one defrauded.

In a voluntary trade, each party has to receive what it bargained for. If one side offers real grapes but delivers fake grapes, then it's fraud, not trade.

Repeating our premise, with some added precision now that it has matured to a conclusion: in every voluntary trade, where each party gets what they bargained for, the trade by definition increases the individual wealth of each of the parties at the moment of the trade.

What about the overall wealth of society, though? Our statement went beyond individual wealth, and said that voluntary trades also increase the overall wealth of society. This conclusion becomes more clear when we answer two primary objections: trades that harm third parties, and trades that didn't really increase society's wealth even though they made the parties happier.

First, let's deal with the third party objection - what about a trade between two parties that hurts a third party? Farmer Fred pays Builder Bill to build a barn, and the barn blocks Neighbor Ned's view. We can believe that Fred and Bill both consider themselves better off, but what about poor Ned? Didn't the Fred/Bill trade harm Ned, and thus decrease Ned's wealth? We have to consider several possibilities here.

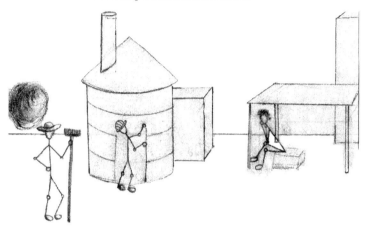

What happens when Farmer Fred hires Builder Bill to build a barn, and the barn blocks Neighbor Ned's view? Did the Fred/Bill trade decrease Ned's wealth?

If Fred and Ned had an earlier trade where Fred promised not to block Ned's view, then Fred is taking away something already promised to Ned, and Ned has a claim against Fred for a failure to deliver what was promised (a claim that Fred has committed theft or fraud). If Fred can fairly compensate Ned, then everyone's participation in the trade is voluntary, and the total wealth of all is increased. If Fred does not fairly compensate Ned, than Ned's loss of wealth is not due to any voluntary transaction in money, but rather to Fred's failure to deliver on his earlier promise to Ned.

44

If there was not a "no view blocking" agreement between Ned and Fred, then it is not correct to lay the blame for Ned's wealth decrease on the Fred/Bill deal. Even though the Fred/Bill deal can be pointed to as the event that triggered the decrease in Ned's wealth, the blocking of Ned's view by a building on Fred's land was an event that was possible before the barn was built. If an event that is possible eventually happens, then it is akin to the passage of time causing the decrease. As a simpler example, Fred bought a cow, and several years later it dies. Whose fault is the decrease in Fred's wealth by one cow? It was not the purchase of the cow. It was just the passage of time, the occurrence of events that are allowed to happen. When Ned bought his porch, what did he get? He traded money for a porch with a view, but it was really a porch with a view that could be blocked by a future building.

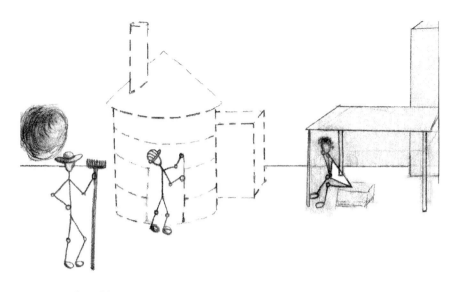

If Ned had already accepted the risk that a future barn might block his view, Ned's decrease in wealth is caused by the passage of time that allowed the risk to become reality. The trade between Fred and Bill is not to blame.

After the Fred/Bill deal, Ned still has exactly what he had before, except that the risk of the view getting blocked has now become 100%. This gets more complex in real life contract law, of course, but the dispute will be over the specifics of Ned's original deal - whether Fred promised to never block Ned's view. The lawsuit will be about whether Ned acquired a promise that his view would not be blocked. The Fred/Bill barn deal is not the issue, and the Fred/Bill deal increased the wealth of Fred and Bill, and did not decrease the wealth of Ned.

Even if effects on third parties are accounted for, we've all seen people waste money. How can those deals increase the wealth of society? How can lots of people buying pet rocks increase the wealth of society? We are just wasting money (acquired by trade for our time) on things that are not really valuable. This looks like a reasonable objection, but on closer inspection it ends up either back at the starting point, or at a theological argument.

The statement about increasing the wealth of society assumes that the wealth of society can be determined by simply summing up the wealth of all the individuals. With that assumption, anything that increases the wealth of each of the individuals involved must also increase the sum of the wealth of all the individuals. So the "wasting money" objection requires that we make some objective statement about the wealth of society, specifically a statement that the wealth of society is something different than the aggregation of the wealth of all the individuals. The measure we proposed was to take each individual's estimation of his own wealth, and then add up all those estimations. Now, we are really not trying to quantify and add them all up; we are just using that to assess whether a voluntary trade between two parties increases the aggregate wealth. If there is to be some other valuation, then there must be some measure of an individual's wealth that is more accurate than the measure assigned by the individual himself. Where can such a measure be found?

You could say that you know how much everything is truly worth to every person, and that your knowledge of the true worth trumps each person's individual estimation. Since all things are different, and all people are different, you would be tasked with knowing how 8 billion people should value each of the possible things in the world at each instant of time. That's a bit much for anyone to manage, even if you are right. And, why should your valuation be the one that matters?

You can assert that there is an objective measure of wealth, such as how much money people have. We've already shown that money by itself has no value, so a measure using money would immediately run into the question of how to translate money into real wealth, and translate wealth or things back into money. But we know that different people place different values on money and things, else there would be no trades. A hungry person will gladly trade water for food, and a thirsty person will be made wealthier by making the trade. So trying to assess aggregate wealth based on money leaves out the critical element - how each person values things, or money that can be translated into things.

You can assert that the real measure is how happy people are. How would you attempt to measure each person's happiness? And is happiness really the catch-all measure? What about contentment, or security, or excitement? Those mean different things to different people, so the only way to make such a measure is to let each person express his own weighted combination, and then communicate it. But that's just what our individual measure does – people can trade money for contentment, or security, or excitement, according to each person's individual valuation.

Maybe there is an objective value, outside the realm of human expertise. You are now appealing to some extra-human standard, which runs you into a whole basket of theological arguments. That might be the real measure, but we don't have any agreed way to assess that, and, since each person will have their own view of what is the right measure, we circle right back to our individual measures.

So, each trade increases the wealth of each party, as measured by that party. Each trade therefore also increases the aggregate wealth of the society including those parties.

We have one more class of objection to deal with. We've seen or read of people with lots of money who are miserable. The Bible even says that money is the root of all evil. What about those? I said that money always makes people better off, so am I arguing against the Bible?

We need to be careful with our wording, here. First, the Bible quote is from 1 Timothy 6:10, and actually says that the **love** of money is **a** root of all **kinds** of evil. So saying "money does good" is not in conflict with the Bible's teaching that the love of money can be bad. Second, we didn't say that **money** always makes people better off, but rather that **voluntary trades** always make people better off. Money enables a tremendous expansion of the types of voluntary trades we can make - different sizes, different times, different places, different trading partners.

More voluntary trades available means more opportunities to increase wealth. People who love money, or who devote themselves to storing money, do not disprove the original statement. The trade is the substance; the money is just the intermediate form. People who love money are focusing on the intermediate form, and not the substance. Collecting the intermediate form does not get you the benefits of the substance. Observing that collectors of currency can be miserable doesn't say anything about whether trades using money make people better off.

Consider sportsman Sam and lazy Larry. Sam loves to play a sport, and realizes all the benefits from the exercise, the competition, the thrill of victory, the fellowship of a team. Sam wins a competition, and is awarded a trophy. The trophy represents all the other stuff that came before it. Larry sees Sam's trophy, and wants all the benefits that Sam got on the way to winning the trophy. So Larry goes to the trophy store and buys 10 trophies. Is Larry 10 times happier than Sam? No, the trophies can be representations of value, but are not themselves valuable. This is not the trophies' fault, however. In a similar way, money (someone else's promise to do something) and currency (a marker that represents money) can be representative of value, but are not by themselves valuable.

Money is at most only a temporary store of value. It has no value sitting still; it has to be in motion in trades for the value to be realized.

To keep in mind:
1. Wealth is a measure on how closely the world conforms to your desire for it to be.
2. Voluntary trades increase the wealth of everyone, as measured by each person's individual determination of wealth.
3. Money enables a dramatic expansion in the kinds of voluntary trades that can be made, and so money makes it easier to increase everyone's wealth.

FOUNDATION #4. MONEY IS ONLY CREATED BY TRADING VALUE FOR UNIVERSALLY TRUSTED PROMISES.

The money supply and the currency supply are different. The money supply exactly matches the total of trusted promises. This statement probably sounds obscure, but this is an important principle to understand. The difference between the supply of money and the supply of currency is one of the least understood aspects of money, and failure to understand this has caused severe money problems throughout history. Many long and complicated books have been written about managing the money supply, and no government on earth has ever gotten it consistently right. People feel trapped and powerless, and societies have fallen, because people did not understand that creating **currency** is not the same as creating **money**.

Earlier, we set up some definitions of money and currency. We should have a pretty good understanding of money now. Money is a unit of promise, tradeable as a placeholder among a large enough group of people that people accept the promise as universal. Since money as a concept has no physical existence, we establish currency to represent money. Currency can take **any** form: printed bills, coins, digital entries in computer systems, or big rocks in the middle of town. All that is necessary for a valid currency is that enough people accept it as representing real money.

So let's think about what the "money supply" means, using these definitions. Each unit of money represents someone's promise to do something for someone else. Paul gave Adam a peach, and Adam gave Paul a promise. Each time someone makes a promise, some money is created. Well, not quite – for a promise to count as money, it has to be a promise that everyone in the relevant society will accept in trade for real services.

How can we tell whether Questionable Quincy in front of us can make a promise that we should trust? We ask everyone else – if Quincy has provided services that justified someone else giving Quincy a universal promise (some money), then we'll accept that universal promise (money) that Quincy is holding. For us to trust Quincy, he first has to provide something that someone will accept in trade for an unquestioned, universal promise. Quincy has to provide something real so that someone else will give him money for it. The risk in trusting Quincy is borne by the person who receives Quincy's real contribution and gives money in exchange.

This leads to our statement: the total amount of money in a society is the total of the promises that everyone is willing to accept. This is independent of the currency used to represent the promises. It is affected by things like the productivity of the people, their optimistic or pessimistic view of the future, and their trust in the rest of society. It is not set by the currency.

We are not just splitting hairs here. If currency represents money, then why is it so important to make a distinction between money and currency? It is important because without that distinction people gradually believe that currency **is** money, instead of just a convenient way of **representing** money.

To see the distinction between currency and money, consider the game of soccer. In the U.S., some complain that soccer games are too low scoring. Games can end 0-0, and a 4-3 score is a high scoring game. Pretend we wanted to address this, and so we take the simple step of making each goal worth 7 points. High scoring games are now 28-21. Have we answered the complaint? Not really: changing the units doesn't change the real thing. The event that matters is scoring the goal; the points are an arbitrary assignment of a numeric value to the event. Money corresponds to the goal-scoring event; the markers or currency are just an adopted convention for assigning a numeric value to the event.

This seemingly tiny disconnect between money and currency can be exploited by people trying to get something for nothing. The obvious route is by counterfeiting money, or, more precisely, by counterfeiting currency. Print some counterfeit currency, and everyone accepts it as money, and you get the benefit of money without having to do anything to support the money. If you counterfeit just a little currency, maybe no one notices and everything keeps working. If there is enough counterfeit currency, though, eventually people's trust in currency starts to fail, and then money (and all it's wealth-maximizing benefits) disappears since there is no trusted way to keep track of how many promises you have made or accepted. We'll talk much more about this in a little bit, but for now just have firmly fixed in your mind the distinction between money and currency. Manipulations in currency do not manipulate money, except to the extent the manipulations in currency affect people's trust in the relationship between money and currency.

Now that we have these key principles well understood, we can look at what they mean in real life.

To keep in mind:
1. **Money must be backed by trustworthy promises of future actions.**
2. **Creating currency does not create money.**
3. **Currency that is not backed by trustworthy promises is counterfeit.**
4. **Too much counterfeit currency destroys the trust that is the basis of money.**
5. **When the trust is gone, the money is gone.**

BUILDING ON THE
FOUNDATIONS OF MONEY

The foundation of money is that it represents trust in the reliability of the promises of other people in the society, and is an enabler of the free trade of promises across different size transactions and at different times and places. Money is effective only on people, and is effective only as long as enough people are willing to believe it is effective. It allows the voluntary ordering of our relationships, without force, and voluntary trades using money uniformly make people more wealthy. Money is separate from currency. That separation is hard to keep in everyone's minds at once, so manipulations in currency can have drastic effects on people's confidence in money.

Now that we understand the foundations of money, we can build our understanding of how money works in the world. First we'll look at three ways people try to create money without first creating the value that money represents – government printing, government borrowing, and fractional reserve banking – and see how they create currency, but not money. We'll look at some examples from history of the disasters that follow from disconnecting currency from money. Since creating currency doesn't create money, we'll look at how a person, or a people, can get more money. Last, we'll look at some common arguments against money and riches, and reason about which are valid and what to do about them.

WHAT HAPPENS WHEN A GOVERNMENT TRIES TO PRINT MONEY?

If money is a universally accepted promise, and currency is just an agreed-upon representation of those promises, then why does the government have any role in money?

It's a gradual evolution. When money first starts, the people using the money agree on the markers for money: big rocks standing in the middle of town, coins with the mark of some trusted financial institution, or paper issued by the government. Just as people try to cheat on services (work fewer than the full hours, deliver less than the full amount), people try to cheat on currency. It can be a lot easier to make some fake currency than to earn real currency.

Trading fake markers, or counterfeit currency, is a transaction by fraud (since real currency was promised but fake currency was delivered) and thus government action is appropriate. At first, the government might just make it criminal to shave the edges of coins, or to use faulty weights or measures. Usually, the government eventually ends up certifying all markers, by taking control over the currency. The only official markers for money are those produced by the government. This can be a great benefit, since the collective trust in currency as a representation of money is enhanced. Everyone trusts that a government-issued currency really corresponds to real money, and will be trusted by everyone else. People can still try to use their private markers, but not everyone trusts them since the government will not back up a claim of cheating using those private markers. So far, government involvement in money seems reasonable, and necessary, and good.

Government control of the markers for money is the nose of the camel under the tent, however. Government certification of valid markers is a useful service, and an important safeguard against fraud. However, governments never stop at certifying the validity of markers; they always tinker with the number of markers available. Recall that for a marker to count as real money, the marker has to represent a promise for future services. When the government controls the markers and can create new ones, however, it can create markers out of thin air.

The government markers do not represent promises acquired in exchange for delivery of real services, and thus they do **not** correspond to actual money. The total markers for money goes up, but the total money does not. A simple illustration can help make this clear.

Let's assume we have 100 units of trustworthy promises outstanding, and 1000 markers. One unit of promise corresponds to 10 markers. Now the government creates 100 new markers. Creation of new markers has not changed the number of promises though. To have one unit of promise now, you have to have 11 markers. The government has just taken

10% of the wealth of everyone who has money, without taxation, force, or even getting noticed.

This might seem a little obscure, but look at what would happen if we changed the names. Instead of government creating new markers, let's print some of our own. We now have 100 new markers, acquired by printing them instead of trading them for services. We are counterfeiters, subject to punishment for theft. How is that different from the government operation? At its root, it is not.

But doesn't the government have to control the money supply? Otherwise prices would go up, or go down, or do something else we don't like. We need the government to control how much money is in circulation to help dampen market swings, don't we? Do we?

How does government control of the money supply work, on a fundamental level? Staying consistent to our terminology, the government is not really controlling the money supply. Money is the unit of promises for future human action. The government doesn't control the total capacity for human action, or the reliability of people's promises to act (except in extreme cases like imprisoning everyone). So what the government is really controlling is not the supply of money, but rather the supply of markers for money, or the currency supply. Does controlling the supply of currency do anything?

When the government increases or decreases the "money supply," it is really just changing the units of the markers or currency. If a hamburger costs 10 minutes of time working at a particular job, it will cost the same 10 minutes regardless of whether those 10 minutes are priced at one dollar or one million dollars. Money is just an intermediate form for translation between real things, so the units are not relevant. Prices denominated in a currency are meaningless; it is only when those prices in a currency are translatable into other real things that the prices have meaning. It is inconvenient to price silk fabric in units of pork bellies, so currency makes a very good, universal intermediate form.

It is relevant, however, how people perceive the value of the currency, the markers for money. Since money gets it value only from people's confidence in it, people's perception is critical. It's kind of the ultimate popularity contest. If the units change slowly enough, then people have the chance to slowly change their expectations and no significant disruption is realized. That is one reason why governments try to keep inflation fairly low. As long as it is not too high, people don't complain too much. If the government only steals 3-5% of your money every year by printing money, maybe you don't mind too much. But the effect of government creating markers is actually even worse than the stated inflation rate, since the government increase in supply of currency also siphons off some of the benefit we should realize from increasing technology and productivity.

To get a clear look at the principle, we have to simplify things a bit. Assume an economy where everyone produces one unit of output per day, and consumes a total of seven units every week. There are various voluntary trades to make the seven units/week work out for everyone, but we've normalized productivity and consumption to make the math easy and the illustration simple. Let's set the initial supply of currency such that each unit of output is represented by one currency unit. Everyone works, and earns one currency unit per day, and spends seven currency units per week, or an average of one currency unit per day.

Everyone takes a course in "how to work smarter," and soon everyone is producing 10 units per day. We all enjoy the fruits of our increased productivity, and expand our consumption so that now everyone consumes an average of 70 units per week. So far so good. Everyone is increasing his or her wealth ten times as rapidly as before. What happens if there is no change to the supply of currency? We have 10 times as many goods, but the same number of points. Each good is worth, in currency units, 1/10th of what it used to. As our productivity improved, everyone found prices declining (same currency spread over more stuff) - prices paid for their output declined and prices they paid for output from others declined at the same rate.

We get a different result, though, if the government increases the supply of currency so that prices don't change. We need 10 times as much currency as originally. But everyone's output translates to 10 units of currency per day, and everyone's consumption translates to 10 units of currency per day. Seems like everyone is even, and all the government expansion has done is helped keep prices stable. How has the government expansion hurt anyone?

The key is to look at what happened to accomplish the expansion. When the productivity first increased from one unit per day to two units per day, the government had to double the currency in circulation. The government didn't just give the currency to everyone - in a realistic example, there would be no way to determine exactly how much of the new currency each person should get since productivity gains would not be uniform as in our simplified example. The government printed the currency, then used the new markers to induce private actions. Maybe the government used them to pay government workers, in which case they were an unnoticed tax. Maybe the government gave them to poor people, in which case they were a forced act of charity funded by an invisible tax. Maybe the government used them to buy stuff, in which case they were another unnoticed tax.

In any case, when government first doubled the currency in circulation, the government took half a day's labor from everyone, without anyone noticing. This was repeated through all the productivity gains. The price per unit stays constant, so there would be no inflation reported. However, the actual purchasing power of the currency, in terms of human output, is now 1/10 of the original value. You used to be able to buy one day's output for one currency unit; now you need 10 currency units to buy one day's output.

In fairness to the government, provision of a valid and trustable currency is a valuable service, a value that can be rightfully traded for money. It can be debated whether the government providing currency that is hard to counterfeit, and punishing counterfeiters, should be paid by taxes or just by government printing a little extra currency. In our example, and throughout history, governments meddle in currency far more than just what is justified by the value added by government providing a trustable currency.

But why would the government do such a thing? Wouldn't a good government just be content with punishing the bad act of counterfeiting? Why would a government dilute its people's money (their mutual promises) by issuing new currency?

The power of money historically proves irresistible to governments. Working from the foundations of money, let's analyze how governments abuse the power to control currency. How do the people in government get the rest of society to behave? Punishing wrong actions is a powerful tool for preventing action, but poor at inducing particular new actions. If you want to induce a specific action, you have to offer a reward. The most efficient way of offering a reward is to use money. Money as a reward is particularly effective since it allows the recipient to choose the type of reward that is most valuable to him. But how does government get money to use as rewards?

The answer starts with a necessary intersection of government and money. In its foundation, government is based on a collective right to use force against individuals. But it is unwieldy for any large society to always act collectively. Gathering everyone together to go catch a thief is a pretty large cost - everyone has to stop normal work to participate in this one task, and we can only do one government task at a time, and we are not all equally well suited to catch thieves. So we immediately need to deputize individuals to do the tasks desired by the group. We induce those individuals to act by offering money. But where do we get the money? Well, since it's a collective act that we want the individuals to perform, we collect the money from everyone. Everyone pays their share, and then we use that money to hire the people to act as government on everyone's behalf. At first you just need to pay the sheriff. Then you have to pay the deputy, and then the jailer, and then the people to build and maintain the jail. Eventually you have to pay tax collectors to go and collect the contributions from everyone to pay for the sheriff and the deputy and the jail builders.

At this point, government is functioning. It is doing what everyone wants it to do, and collecting only the money required to do that. We have collectively and forcibly imposed taxes, which is effectively the rule that "if you live here and you do not pay your share of the expense in punishing wrongdoers, then we will punish you." People might press for expansion of government power, for example to make laws catch up to new technologies or new ideas in crime. However, expansion in what government has to do means an increase in taxes from everyone.

People don't like being pressed into service, which is in principle what happens with taxes. Remember money represents only a promise of future service, so a tax paid in money is effectively the same as a tax paid by forced servitude. Since people resist taxes, there is a built in give and take with government expansion paid by taxes. At this level of function, the role of government is generally self-limiting due to the correlation with taxes. It may change over time as the society desires more or less from government, but the change is always trending toward a balance of the competing desires for more government and less taxes. It is a roughly voluntary trade on the part of the citizens - if they want more government, then they have to pay for it. That trade is part of the common experience – you make your choices and you pay your prices.

People being people, and wanting something for nothing, and wanting to tell other people how to live, there will still be a demand for more government action. Small groups highly affected by an issue will lobby for expanded government action in areas that have relatively small effects on others. A $100 government expansion that helps one person, balanced against a one penny effect on lots of people, will motivate the one in support but not the many in opposition. Also, some in government will try to increase their power or security. Opposition to enforced service (taxes) resists government expansion, but we have seen that governments expand anyway. What happens?

In the real world, the government creates currency to soak up all the increase in productivity, plus some. The "plus some" is the official inflation rate. In the United States, the official inflation rate killed about 96% of the value of a dollar from 1913 to 2013. The government siphoned off 96% of the wealth in the country as represented by 1913 dollars, without much resistance. Over the same time period, the productivity of the US worker has increased at a comparable rate. All of that productivity was also siphoned off by increases in the currency in circulation. The government printed money markers to soak up a 23-fold increase in productivity, and still took another 96% out of the country's wealth. And that's purely from currency creation; it doesn't count taxes, fees, and regulations.

To be fair, the government didn't just burn the wealth it siphoned off. However, by definition voluntary trades always increase individual wealth. Trade with the government is usually tainted by force (since you don't get to choose whether you pay taxes), or by fraud (since you are convinced to accept the government's new currency as though it represented real money). Also, we've seen many examples of waste, fraud, abuse, and incompetence in government. It is hard for an individual to waste and defraud on the scale of government waste and fraud, since every individual transaction requires a voluntary participant on the other side. Voluntary participants, looking out for their own interests, are good at avoiding fraud. It's very hard for any individual to have a noticeable impact on any government trade, however, given the size of the government and the involuntary nature of transactions with the government.

Bad as it is, this siphoning of wealth is not the most dangerous part. More dangerous than a little government inflation today is the ultimate result of the lack of any real check on the government's ability to do it. The ability to lay claim to the output of other people, with no work on your part, is irresistible. It's the root of slavery, and of robbery and of fraud. The only remedy is to prohibit it and to punish those who engage in it. But, when the government does it, the only remedy is not available. We have the fox guarding the henhouse.

Throughout history, many countries have failed because of the collapse of money, which comes from the universal appeal of getting something for nothing. It's not always a popular topic, but government currency-printing played a key role in many famous collapses.

The problems of the Roman empire.

Roman emperors had to have money to pay the troops. Emperors were made and unmade (killed) by the army, so the emperor had to be sure he had enough money to pay them well enough to stay loyal to him. After the Roman citizens' ability to pay taxes was tapped out, the empire increased inheritance taxes, then expanded the tax base by making everyone citizens. This was still not enough, so successive emperors devalued the currency to generate enough currency to keep the army happy.

The basic currency in the first and second centuries AD was a silver denarius, introduced by Augustus. It was originally 95% silver. Within about 100 years, emperors had changed it to only 50% silver, effectively doubling the currency in circulation. In our soccer analogy, scores were now twice what they were before, even though no more goals were being scored. A similar devaluation affected the gold-based coins as well.

This was effectively theft of one half the value of money - people trusted yesterday's coin, and the emperor's new diluted coins had a short time to trade off that previous trust. Half the value was enough to cause problems, but not enough to satisfy the appetite for more. Before the end of this period, the "silver" denarius had only 0.5% silver. 99.5% of the value of the people's trust in the currency as representative of real money had been taken by the government. By the end of the third century, the "silver" denarius was a bronze coin quickly dipped in silver. A new silver coin was introduced, and within a decade it too was devalued by 50%. A new gold currency was introduced, initially at 50 thousand gold denarii per pound of gold. In 38 years, it was 20 million denarii per pound of gold. Eventually, the currency was so undependable that gold coins had to be melted into bullion before the government would accept payment - even the government didn't trust government currency!

This failure of currency led to all manner of problems. The government insisted taxes be paid in real goods instead of its own rapidly failing currency. People tried to evade those taxes, even by quitting their jobs or farms, so the government made it became illegal to leave your farm or trade. You were bound to the land or occupation you currently had. Farmers and tradesmen still left their occupations when they died, however, which caused a problem for the government. So the government made children also bound to the farm or trade of their parents. The Roman government's attempt to recover from its own currency debasement resulted in Roman citizens eventually becoming serfs, tied to forced servitude on land with no hope for them or their children.

Tax collectors, called decurions, were made personally liable for taxes they could not collect. Since the taxes were uncollectable due to the rapidly changing currency, the position of decurion was not very desirable. Decurions resigned until that was made illegal, then they fled in the night. When caught, they were forcibly restored to their official positions. One emperor even gave Christians an out - they could avoid execution by becoming a decurion. The battle over control of "free" money was also waged in the halls of power - during the third century AD, there were about 26 emperors; only one died a natural death.

The full tale of the fall of the Roman empire is the subject of many books, but it is clear that the government was unable to resist the temptation of free money. Falling to that temptation destroyed the economic viability of the society.

The disaster of the French Revolution.

The French Revolution started with excessive government spending, was made worse by government creation of currency, and eventually destroyed France's economy, society, and many of its people.

Louis XVI's opulent lifestyle could not be sustained by revenue from taxation, so he convened the Estates General in 1789 to vote him more money. They refused, the Parisian mob stormed the Estates General and then the Bastille, and the revolution was on. Within 2 years, Louis XVI was beheaded. 2 years later, Robespierre, one of the leaders of the revolution, was beheaded. Within 5 years, France was under the dictatorship of Napolean. What happened? A series of steps, each taking a bigger bite of the temptation for government to "create" money by printing currency.

One of the first steps the revolutionary government took to get more money was to seize the assets of the church, chiefly the lands owned by the church. This was no subtle confiscation by inflation; it was just a straightforward taking. If you weren't the church, though, you didn't complain. But what to do with all that property? It takes management and time to make money from farmland, and the government wanted money now. You could sell it, but to whom? And what would happen to prices if you flooded the market with all that land?

As too often happens, the solution was to print some currency. The government created the assignat: a paper currency that was supposedly backed by the value of the land seized from the church. When the government eventually sold the land, it would redeem the assignat currency for some currency that represented real money. The assignat was thus a promise to trade a piece of printed paper for real money later.

The first assignats appeared to be a great success. New currency always appears to mean new wealth. Everyone has an intuition about the correspondence between currency and money: how much an assignat (or dollar) will buy. So when new assignats (or dollars) show up, everyone feels richer even though the wealth behind the total currency has not changed. But people's built-in intuition gradually gets adjusted to match reality - prices rise, people adjust. When people begin expecting prices to rise, the process rapidly gets out of control. In France, the first 400 million livres of assignats were printed in early 1789. The temptation of free money proved too hard to resist - 800 million more were issued in September 1789, then more in June 1791, December 1791, and April 1792. So many assignats were printed that the currency was no longer translatable to money, so the people's trust in trade was gone, and society rapidly fell apart.

The government tried to regain control of money - barter was outlawed, price controls were established, and failure to obey the non-barter laws was a capital offense. More and more assignats were issued; by 1795 45 billion assignats were in circulation. The old currencies were worthless, and the supply of assignats had grown over 100-fold in just a few years.

What does a government do when the people no longer trust the currency? The French government (like others before and since) just started over. They destroyed the plates for printing assignats, and issued a new currency. The mandat replaced the assignat at a rate of 30 to 1. Changing the units doesn't cure the temptation to inflation, though. Within about a year the mandat was worth only 3% of its original value. By the next year, the assignat and mandat were both declared no longer legal tender.

Even though the correspondence of currency to money is arbitrary, there has to be some correspondence that is widely accepted or the money dies. What happened when there was no currency that could be trusted to represent money?

Napolean came home, made himself dictator, and issued hard-to-counterfeit coins. People regained their trust that currency was translatable to real money, and the productivity and trade that currency printing had destroyed came back full speed. Money was restored, but at the cost of submission to a dictatorship, and years of Napoleanic wars with their millions of dead all across Europe.

Wheelbarrows of the Weimar republic.

Germany financed its participation in the First World War by borrowing. The heavy government borrowing was a form of currency debasement; the government was just promising to supply marks later rather than printing them today. During the war, the mark fell steadily from about 4.2 marks per dollar to about 9 marks per dollar.

After the war, Germany was forced to pay reparations to the victors. Those reparations had to be paid in hard currency (backed by gold), not paper marks. The German government did not have enough gold, and it couldn't print marks to pay the reparations. So the German government printed marks anyway, and traded them for other currencies. They relied on the time lag between today's prices and tomorrow's newly printed marks to push their debts onto their trading partners. Each day the new, debased marks could be used to buy other currencies at yesterday's prices. This of course led to a very rapid expansion in the supply of paper marks. The result? In 1919, one US dollar bought about seven German marks. Four years later, one US dollar bought over four trillion German marks. People needed wheelbarrows to carry their daily pay to the markets, and you had to spend before the next day's inflation wiped out the value of today's pay. The mark as a currency was worthless; it no longer had any correlation to real money.

In Germany's case, the forces to debase the currency were largely external. However, under the press of a need for more money to pay debts, the German government did the same thing every government does - it printed more currency. The necessary, real solution was to make more real money, meaning, have the people's promises for services be worth more. Instead, the government just changed the currency units. Just as in our sports analogy, changing the number of points awarded for a goal did not change the number of goals.

There are many reasons for Hitler's rise to power, and the death and destruction brought by the Second World War. Like with France and Napoleon, the economic, social, and political breakdown that ensued from the death of money certainly played a large role in preparing the people to accept a strongman ruler.

When we give the government the power to create currency out of thin air, we have given the government the power to call on our services in any amount and at any time. The government now has a backdoor route to as much money as it wants. The government-created money is not backed by anything from the government, but rather steals from our trust in each other's promises. It's like the cowbird, who lays its eggs in the nests of other birds. The cowbird gets all the benefits, but doesn't have to supply any of the work.

To keep in mind:

1. **Government control of currency can help sustain the trust that is necessary for money to exist.**
2. **Government control of currency can allow government to become an unaccountable counterfeiter, and history proves that the temptation to counterfeit is too great for government to resist.**
3. **The government's ability to create currency becomes a government's ability to destroy trust among people, and ultimately to destroy the society.**

GOVERNMENT BORROWING MONEY IS THE SAME AS GOVERNMENT PRINTING CURRENCY.

Reason shows that government cannot create money. Government can create currency, and that created currency steals real money from real people. History shows that when governments do this, disaster follows. Is there no way that governments can fund their operations other than simple taxes?

When a government wants to spend more than it collects in taxes, and it can't create currency, then it usually borrows. The US government does both, at levels so high they seem not in the real world. What effect does government borrowing have on money?

We need to understand what borrowing is before we can figure out what government borrowing does. In a straight barter transaction, goods are traded for goods. Adam gives an apple, and gets a peach in return. In our usual money transaction, money is traded for goods. Paul gives a peach, and gets money in return. The money is a promise of future services, that Paul expects will be honored by pretty much anyone in society.

Let's extend our line of reasoning to borrowing. When someone borrows an apple from Adam, Adam gives an apple and receives a promise from the borrower to return the apple. Adam has received an individual promise in return for his apple. It gets a little more abstract when the thing loaned is money, but the reasoning holds.

Lenny the lender has some money. Bob the borrower wants to borrow it. Lenny loans it to Bob, and Bob promises to pay it back later. We are ignoring for now all the peripheral matters such as interest rate, security, payment timing, etc. Those don't change the underlying principles, so we will continue to ignore them in this story. We do want to look at exactly what each party gave and got. Lenny had money, which is a promise of unspecified future services that everyone in society trusts will be honored by anyone in society. Lenny gave that to Bob. What did Bob have? Nothing. So what did Bob give Lenny? Bob's promise to give Lenny money in the future. How will Bob get that money (without force or fraud)? Bob will have to provide something of value to one or more people in society. So Bob's promise to Lenny is that Bob will do something valuable later, and give Lenny the money that Bob gets.

Borrowing money is just trading universal promises for individual promises. Lenny gives Bob a general note representing a universal promise (money). Bob gives Lenny a particular note representing Bob's individual promise to Lenny.

We still haven't answered the question – what did Lenny get from Bob? Lenny had money, a promise of future services, redeemable from anyone in the whole society. He received an individual promise from Bob. And what was Bob's individual promise to Lenny? That Bob would provide future services to someone in the general pool of society, so Bob could get money to give to Lenny. Lenny gave away Lenny's money-based ability to get services from anyone Lenny chooses, and received Bob's individual promise to provide services to anyone Bob chooses. Lenny used to have a right to trade for work from anyone; now he just has the right to demand that a particular person, Bob, work for someone.

Let's look at Bob's promise to Lenny a bit closer. If Bob is a dependable guy, whose services are in high demand by everyone, then Lenny may be able to trade Bob's promise in the general marketplace. Bob's promise is like the negotiable instrument we discussed earlier. Remember how we built up the principles of money – promises from someone of future services, that the recipient can trade among the general population. If Lenny can trade Bob's promise of repayment among the general population, then Lenny received money from Bob. So the transaction was just money from Lenny for a negotiable instrument from Bob. There is more risk from Bob's individual negotiable instrument, though, since it doesn't already have the universal acceptability that Lenny's money does (we assumed universal acceptability when we said Lenny had "money"). So Lenny wants more of Bob's individual negotiable instrument than Lenny gives in universal money. That "more" is generally addressed by charging interest.

What if Lenny can't trade Bob's promises to anyone? Then Lenny has traded a universal promise from everyone for an individual promise from Bob. Lenny has to set a value on Bob's individual promise to work in the future. If Bob's promise was to work for Lenny, then Lenny has to discount for the probability that **Lenny** will want what Bob produces. Since Bob's promise was to give money to Lenny, Lenny just has to discount for the probability that **someone** will want what Bob produces.

How does this work when a government borrows? The government is Bob in our example – the government gets a universally acceptable promise now, and gives an individual promise to return money in the future. The individual promise is really a promise to work in exchange for universal promises (money) in the future. What does it mean for a government to issue an individual promise to acquire money in the future?

Let's go back to Lenny and Bob. Maybe Lenny doesn't quite trust Bob, so he insists that Carl co-sign Bob's deal. Carl promises that, if Bob doesn't pay back the money, Carl will pay it back. Translating through the foundations of money, Lenny now has a promise that Bill **or** Carl will work in the future. Lenny has traded his money (a promise drawn on everyone) for a promise drawn on just two guys.

Extend this to government borrowing, and we can see what happens. The government issues an individual promise to provide money in the future. But the government is an abstraction, and can't actually do work to earn money. So who cosigns for the government? Everyone in the domain of that government. The government's "individual" promise is really a promise of everyone in the domain of the government, so the individual borrower's promise when made by the government is really a universal promise. Since government borrowing is backed up by everyone in the society, the document evidencing that promise to repay has all the characteristics of money. The government is creating currency, although with a different look and feel from that usually carried in wallets. Government borrowing steals from the real money produced by real people on the same principle that government printing currency steals real money from real people.

There is one variation that we have to cover a little more precisely. What happens if a government borrows money in a currency that is not controlled exclusively by that government? For example, Poor-Country borrows money from Rich-Country, denominated in Rich-Country's currency. Poor-Country is making a universal promise, at least universal among the people of Poor-Country. But the promise is not to work for people in Poor-Country, but rather to work for people in Rich-Country. From our Lenny and Bob story, it is as though Bob promised to earn the money by working for someone whose name started with "L" (or any other subgroup that corresponded with the specific currency that Lenny loaned). So Poor-Country's people have been impoverished not just by their government's creation of currency, but also by their government's selectivity of what money has been promised. The promise Poor-Country made can not be paid from services generally, but only from the services that Rich-Country desires.

To keep in mind:

Government borrowing looks different than government printing currency, but it has the same effect.

BANKS CAN CREATE CURRENCY, TOO, BUT THEY DON'T CREATE MONEY.

Banks are not very popular these days. Bankers are seldom the good guys in a story. The mean bankers took the farm in the old movies. There is no Banker-man superhero. Bankers are usually suits, with cold, heartless bodies inside, who will lend you an umbrella in fair weather and ask for it back when it begins to rain (as Robert Frost put it). Many populist protests are aimed at banks, although the general protest message is something like "the bank has too much money and I don't have enough." Not a very good articulation of principle, or much of a call to action except robbery. Why don't we like banks? As we'll prove later, we should all be happy if someone has lots of money stored in a vault, so disliking banks because they have vaults of money is irrational. In fact, banks don't have vaults of money, and the reason why they don't is the reason we don't like them.

Berthold Brecht said "It is easier to rob by setting up a bank than by holding up a bank clerk." Herein likes the root of our dislike of banks. From our foundations of money, we can reason that the generation of money is admirable (if we rule out force or fraud) since it enables increases in everyone's wealth. Our analysis is founded on the assumption that money is generated by providing something of value to others. Someone gets money by selling apples, or iPhones. But what do bankers do to justify their money? If we can't see the value they provide, then we react as though they must have obtained it by force or fraud. And it's easy to dislike thieves and swindlers.

What modern bankers do to produce money is hard to see. They provide some services, but tracking savings accounts and cashing checks does not seem to be enough to justify the huge piles of money we envision them having. The complicated secret behind banks is fractional reserve banking.

Fractional reserve banking is a somewhat obscure term for a very obscure system, where a central bank (controlled wholly or partially by the government) acts in concert with all the other banks to create currency out of thin air. It's like a semi-private printing press for money. The foundation of money is that it represents someone's promise to provide services, and that each bit of money must be representative of some services provided and traded for. But banks produce money from nothing; fractional reserve banking lets them take a little of your money, play some tricks, and appear to have lots of money. There are arguments why this is a good idea, but there's little wonder that many regard bankers as swindlers.

We've just introduced a lot of complications, and made some unkind allegations against banks. We need to go back to foundations and build up our understanding of banks and money and government so that this all makes sense.

Let's start with real services that a bank could provide. Chester the cheese man works hard one month, and makes a lot of cheese. Chester makes so much cheese that he can't fit it all in his shop. So he goes to Wally the warehouseman and contracts for Wally to store this excess cheese. Wally provides a service, storing the extra cheese. Chester pays him for that service. Chester gets Wally's services, and Wally gets money, which is a promise from Chester and everyone else of some future service worth the same amount of money.

Chester has some cheese he wants to save for later.
Chester pays Wally to store the cheese in Wally's
warehouse, for Chester to retrieve later.

Chester keeps turning out the cheese, and finds a problem with his arrangement with Wally. Chester wants to make enough cheese so that he can take a break from cheese making for a month. He'll just sell the stored cheese while he's on vacation. But he can't take a vacation while he has to be in the shop to sell cheese. And Wally's warehouse might start to get a little rank if we keep the cheese there too long. Chester has to convert that cheese to something he can store.

So Chester sells the cheese for money. Now he doesn't need to store so much cheese, but he does need to keep the money in a safe place, somewhere it won't get lost or stolen, and with someone who will give it back when Chester wants it. Chester contracts with a different kind of warehouse: a money warehouse. Barney the banker has a big strong house, and will store Chester's money in exchange for a small fee. So Chester gets the benefits of Barney's bank for storing money, and Barney gets a little of Chester's money in payment.

Chester has some money he wants to save for later.
Chester pays Barney to store the money in Barney's bank,
for Chester to retrieve later.

So far so good. I don't think anyone would call Barney, Chester, or Wally swindlers. No one would begrudge Wally or Barney a reasonable fee (meaning, whatever Chester will voluntarily pay) for their storage services. The key to Chester's arrangement with Wally is that Wally will not eat the cheese, or sell it for Wally's benefit. Wally has to keep Chester's cheese for Chester, not use it for Wally. The same key principle applies to Chester's arrangement with Barney. Barney can't eat Chester's money, or use it to buy things for Barney. This kind of safe money storage is the service that banks provide that is easy to recognize and understand, but it is not very lucrative for Barney.

To expose the mystery of fractional reserve banking, we have to add the borrowing money plot line to our story. Lenny the lender has a bunch of money; let's assume Lenny got it all through voluntary transactions so we don't have to look down on him for robbery. The day comes when Farmer Fred wants to buy a new tractor. Fred's problem is that the tractor factory will not give Fred a tractor based on only Fred's individual promise to pay. So Fred needs some "universal promises" (money) to pay for his new tractor. Fred goes to Lenny and they make a deal. Lenny will let Fred rent some of Lenny's money. Fred gets to use the money until his new crops are sold, and then Fred will pay Lenny back the money plus a little more money as rent. Still nothing crooked going on – Lenny and Fred entered a voluntary transaction, and Fred paid Lenny for use of something Lenny owned. The fact that thing being rented was money doesn't change the underlying rental trade.

Our problem comes when Lenny wants to expand his lending business. He can keep bootstrapping it – taking the money rental payments from Fred, and adding those to his pile of money that he can lend to the next guy. Lenny gets impatient, though. He wants to grow his business faster, and make the cover of the business magazines. So he looks around for more money to lend. Where can Lenny find money that he could rent out?

Barney's bank has lots of money on the shelves. Lenny could rent out some of the money that is stored in Barney's bank. But Barney doesn't really have lots of money. Barney has a strong building, where he has promised to keep Chester's money safe for Chester.

Think if Wally rented out the cheese Wally was holding for Chester. That would be wrong; Wally has no right to let anyone else have Chester's cheese. What would Chester do if he asked for his cheese and it had bites taken out, or if it was still out on loan when Chester wanted it back?

Chester's money at Barney's place, however, doesn't really get damaged by lending it. Money is a universal promise, so, as long as we use a standardized currency, money is fungible (meaning, one dollar bill is just as good as another). Barney can loan some of Chester's money to Lenny. As long as Barney gets the money back from Lenny before Chester asks for it, Chester will never even notice. Chester thinks he still has his money stored safely at Barney's place. But Barney loaned Chester's money to Lenny, and Lenny loaned that money to others. It's like a shell game - where is the money? Does Chester have it? Or Lenny? Or Barney? Or the people who rented it from Lenny?

Barney's bank is full of currency that represents Chester's money. Lenny pays Barney to let Lenny use the currency temporarily. As long as Lenny returns the currency to Barney's bank before Chester asks Barney for it, Chester never knows that his currency was working extra shifts for Barney and Lenny.

The answer is in the principles of money and currency. Real money is the unit of universal promise that someone will do something. Currency is just the marker that is used to represent money. Barney and Lenny don't have Chester's money; they just have the currency that represents Chester's money. The promises are still owed to Chester. But, since Barney and Lenny have possession of the currency, they can take that currency and fool other people into thinking it's their money. The money belongs to Chester the whole time, but Barney and Lenny have taken the currency that represents Chester's money and used that currency to convince others to treat them as having the money. Since everyone trusts the currency, the real currency/fake money works just the same as real money.

If you trust your car to a garage, and they take it out joyriding, you have a claim against them for conversion (using your property as their own). We use force to punish those who make unlawful use of property belonging to another. That principle would prevent Lenny and Barney's scheme to use Chester's money while he's not looking, except that our government has allowed fractional reserve banking.

Under fractional reserve banking, when you deposit money in a bank, the money legally becomes the bank's money. All you get is a promise from the bank that it will pay you later. So you didn't deposit money in the bank; you loaned money to the bank – you exchanged your universal promises represented by money for individual promises from the bank represented by your account balance. Since the money belongs to the bank, it can loan it out. Of course, the bank can't loan out all the money it got from everyone, or it would have no money on hand when someone wanted to withdraw it. So the bank reserves a fraction of the money deposited to cover the expected daily withdrawals.

Letting a bank treat **your** money as **its** money doesn't seem quite right, but it doesn't look like too big a problem. If you stored your car in a garage, and they listened to the radio, it might not be right but you wouldn't mind too much. You probably wouldn't even mind too much if they drove it around the block, if there was some way to ensure that the car suffered no appreciable wear and tear. Money doesn't suffer any wear and tear from moving around, so maybe it would be ok to let the bank loan your money to others. But with fractional reserve banking, where you think you have money in the bank while the money is actually out on bank business, things get a lot more involved.

Let's deposit $100 into a bank and follow it through the fractional reserve system. You entrust it to Bank One for safekeeping, and the next day they loan out 90% of it. What happens to the $90 loan? It goes to an individual or company, who then trusts it to Bank Two. That bank loans out 90% of the $90, which ends up being deposited in Bank Three, and so on. But what if the borrower doesn't deposit it in a bank, but uses it to buy something? Then the seller has the money, and the seller deposits it in his bank, and the game continues as before. We started with $100 of real money. That $100 is supposedly still in your account in Bank One. And, somehow, that $100 also turned up as $90 in Bank Two. And, it also turned up as $81 in Bank Three. There is only $100 of real money in our example, but Bank One, Two, and Three show $271 of money on their records. Fractional reserve banking has allowed the banks to create multiples of the original currency, which everyone else thinks represents real money.

This is why people don't understand banks, and hence don't quite trust them. We don't mind if Apple or the local grocery store earns money; we can see what they produce in trade for it. But banks have money (currency, really, but everyone accepts it as money) that is not backed by any services. The bank made currency out of nothing. Banker money works like inflation – new currency is created without corresponding promises or value to back it up. People intuitively suspect that something crooked is going on. Government inflation undermines people's trust in currency, which undermines their trust in money, which undermines their trust in each other. Government can get away with a little inflation, but not too much. Banker currency works the same way. When the reserve fraction is too low, then the banks create too much banker currency, and people get upset, though they often don't understand why.

I mentioned before that the government had a role here. If one bank engaged in fractional reserve banking, even if the government allowed it, the bank would still run a huge risk. Every day the bank would have the risk that it would not retain enough cash reserves to satisfy all withdrawal requests. As soon as people thought there might not be enough cash, then everyone would try to get their money out before the bank ran out. This is a "run on the bank," and illustrates the bankruptcy that is always just around the corner with fractional reserve banking. However, the risk of a particular bank's failure is confined to those who trusted that particular bank with their money, so there is an individual motivation to limit fractional reserve banking – people have an incentive to trust their money only to banks that will be careful with it.

However, if the government guarantees deposits, then the government can use its credibility to keep people from fearing for the money's safety. The government doesn't have the cash laying around either, but it can always print some. Also, the risk is not so much that the bank **will** run out of cash, but that people will **worry** that the bank will run out of cash. As long as people don't panic and all try to get their cash at once, the bank can survive. The central bank, under control of the government, keeps people from fearing for their money even though most of their money is out on bank's business and not in the vault. This new banker currency, backed by the government's ability to print unlimited new currency, works just like new currency actually printed by the government except that the bank gets it instead of the government.

The same central bank, with all the other banks that are forced to work together, controls the reserve requirements: the portion of the bank's deposits that it has to actually keep on hand. Assuming that you can get comfortable with the idea of fractional reserve banking, what do you think is a reasonable reserve requirement? How much of your deposit should the bank have ready for you? The other side of this question is how much non-money currency should the bank be able to create for each dollar you trust to them? Most? Half? None?

In the U.S., as of Dec. 2012, the reserve requirement for the first $12 million in deposits in a bank is zero. A reserve requirement of zero means that the bank doesn't have to keep any currency actually in the vault. Each bank can create $12 million in non-money currency from the first $12 million in deposits. Up to $80 million, the reserve requirement is 3%. A bank can create $89.6 million of bank currency from $92 million deposits of real people money in each bank.

But the effect is much greater, since each dollar that is created and loaned out gets deposited in another bank, where the same currency multiplication happens again. With a 0% reserve requirement, the first $12 million can get loaned and re-loaned an infinite number of times, so the only limit to currency creation is the number of banks playing the game. The first $80 million, once loaned out as much as possible subject to a 3% reserve requirement, can give rise to $2.6 billion of non-money currency created by the banks playing the game. What do they have to do to get access to that $2.6 billion? Join the banking system, and accept $80 million in deposits. No wonder it is easier to rob by setting up a bank than by holding up a bank clerk.

There are many solid arguments in favor of fractional reserve banking. Generally, they are based on voluntary lending/borrowing transactions. Those are arguments why banks should be allowed to loan out deposits. They are not arguments for why the government should set the reserve requirement, compel banks to participate in the reserve system, or guarantee deposits. I think it's hard to argue that the government should force you to put your own wealth behind the government's guarantee of everyone else's deposits, or that you should be prohibited from picking between a bank with higher reserves (lower risk) and one with lower reserves (higher risk).

To keep in mind:
1. For those who don't trust banks, now you know why.
2. For those who think banks shouldn't have so much money, now you know how they create it.
3. For those trying to figure out how to create money without working for it, now you know how (I admit that banks provide real services, and it's a lot of work to operate a bank, but the fundamental of fractional reserve banking is the big driver).

EVERY CURRENCY IS A FIAT CURRENCY, BUT NOT ALL FIAT CURRENCIES ARE CREATED EQUAL.

We've seen that governments and banks can produce currency that does not really represent money. People can't distinguish between currency matched with money, and currency that is made out of thin air, so the real money gets diluted. This has been a problem for ages, and, not surprisingly, people have tried to solve it for ages.

One solution is to insist that only "real money" can be used as currency. "Real money" in this context is not as we've defined it; rather, it generally refers to some precious metal, usually gold or silver, which is formed into coins that serve as currency. The argument is that gold and silver are "real money," fundamentally different from all other things used as currency. This is a misunderstanding that obscures some real benefits to gold or silver currencies.

I said before that there was nothing special about precious metals as money. If traded for their intrinsic value, then you have barter transactions. If traded because of trust that others would also trade for them, then they are being used to represent money. They share all the same characteristics as other markers for money; mainly, that they are accepted as money only because everyone believes that everyone else will accept them as money.

Fiat currencies are currencies that are accepted as money just because the government says they are money. The argument is that gold and silver are "real money" and somehow outside the dynamics of fiat currencies. That is not true, however. Anything that enough people accept as representative of money will work as a currency - dollar bills, or rai stones, or pieces of gold. A currency, even a fiat currency, does not become money because a **government** says it is money; it becomes money because **people** trust that **other people** believe it is money. This was true about France's assignats; it is true about paper currency; and it is true about gold and silver. If no one will accept gold in trade, then gold is not useful as currency. Gold and silver are fiat currencies because **all** currencies are fiat currencies. Admittedly, confidence in gold as a currency might be more dependable since it is harder to debase by printing new currency, but its value as money is still wholly dependent on the trust that everyone else also accepts it as money.

But then why have gold and silver been successful as currency? Why have so many successful economies been built on currencies denominated in, or backed by, gold and silver?

Precious metals have a characteristic that makes them especially, but not uniquely, useful as currency. The supply of them is generally somewhat limited. Does this matter? We haven't talked about limited supply having anything to do with money. In fact, if money is the trust of other people's promises, it seems like there could be an unlimited supply of money.

Again, the key is the distinction between money and currency. As we've already seen, the temptation for the government (or banks) to create currency is irresistible. Everyone looks wealthier immediately, since our intuitive correlation between currency and money, between the arbitrary markers for money and the real wealth associated with money, is built over time, based on a given supply of currency. An expansion in the currency available is not immediately reflected in our intuition about value, so we feel wealthier even though we are not. It is not until that inflation erodes the trust that is required for money that we feel poorer. If we see a soccer game with a 9-6 score, we think it was a goal-fest until we adjust to the new correspondence of three points per goal.

This means that it is vital that the government's ability to create currency be constrained. If the government cannot easily create currency, then it has a hard time siphoning off wealth without being noticed. Currency creation can be constrained by the wisdom and self-discipline of those in government, but people are notoriously bad at resisting temptations, and governments are especially bad at foregoing actions that can enhance their power. Currency creation can be constrained by a vigilant citizenry, but citizens generally like what looks like free money, or opportunities to get something for nothing. Currency creation is best constrained by some force not subject to manipulation by government or citizens. The relatively fixed supply of gold and silver, and the difficulty in obtaining more, makes them good candidates for currency. A currency that is exclusively in gold or silver, or any other commodity in limited supply, will be hard to inflate.

It is interesting to look at a modern attempt at this. The BITCOIN currency has gained some popularity as a digital, worldwide currency. BITCOINS are produced by computer solution of time-consuming calculations, so the supply of them increases very slowly. The total number of BITCOINS ever to be produced is said to have a fixed limit. At the first look, BITCOINS cannot be created by any government, and so offer some characteristics desirable in a stable currency.

BITCOINS have some problems, thought. First, remember that currency has value only if enough people believe it represents real money. If your trading partners do not accept BITCOINS, then you will not accept them either. Also, government control of a currency has important benefits: counterfeiting can be treated as a crime, and punished as the fraud or theft that it is. With a currency not controlled by any government, it may be impossible to bring government action (physical punishment) to bear in the prevention of counterfeiting. Also, even though BITCOINS are not controlled by a government, they are controlled by someone. That person (or multiple persons) will have the same temptation to make a few free BITCOINS for themselves. Once started down that road, BITCOINS will devalue just like all other creatable currencies.

Interesting words, but doesn't history prove that gold and silver are so well-suited as currency that they should count as "real money?" Not completely - even gold and silver are subject to debasement, if the right conditions apply. This is illustrated by the price revolution that occurred in Europe in the 16th and 17th centuries. Even though gold and silver were the bases for currency, prices still rose about 600% over 150 years. If gold and silver are real money, and immune to inflationary effects that are part of fiat currencies, then what happened to prices? There were many factors, as always in the real world. One very significant factor, though, was the discovery of the New World.

Spain brought back 170 tons of silver a year from the New World. All that silver resulted in expansion in the units of currency, just as if the Spanish government was silver-plating brass coins as the Romans did. Expanded currency supply did not make people wealthier, even if they initially felt wealthier.

Compare the mining and importation of New World gold and silver to a government that prints dollar bills. The government pays something to produce the new dollars - printing presses, ink, special paper, people to work them. The government then has additional currency that it acquired by the effort of making the currency, but not by the effort of growing apples or pumpkins or doing anything else that actually produces wealth. The government did not produce anything that people inherently want; it produced something (dollar bills) that people only want because it can be traded for things they really want.

Spain was in a similar position. The Spanish government paid to produce the new coins - outfitting ships, paying soldiers, shipping the silver back to Spain, making the silver into coins. The Spanish government then had coins that it could trade for things of real value, but the coins did not start as a representation of the real value or trust that makes money. Rather, the coins only got their value by siphoning off some of the value that was already stored in existing coins. Prices rose, and the Spanish empire fell, because gold and silver coins are fiat currencies just like all other currencies.

To keep in mind:
1. **All currencies, even gold and silver, are by nature fiat currencies.**
2. **All currencies represent money only because everyone believes they represent money.**
3. **The important characteristic of a good currency is that it is hard to create more of it.**

GETTING MORE MONEY – EASY TO UNDERSTAND, NOT EASY TO DO.

With all that we've said about money so far, we still haven't said anything about how to get more of it. This is asked by individuals, and by societies. There are too many possible answers to cover each in detail, but we can look at several approaches.

Recall that the foundation of money is a right to call on others to provide a service. If you have money, you can trade that money for the service of others. Currency is the tangible thing that everyone recognizes as representing money. So one direct route to getting more money is to forget about money and just get more currency. As long as people trust your currency, it is the same as though you had more money. Print some in the basement, and go shopping.

This doesn't work, though, since you're promising real money and delivering only currency. That's fraud, and you will be punished by the government. It is interesting to look at the situation before you get caught, though. It looks like you have more 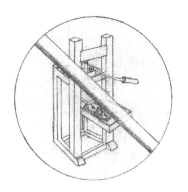 money, but printing your fake currency didn't actually produce more money. Instead, by printing your fake currency you have stolen a fraction of everyone else's real money. The total money is unchanged, but the currency representing it has gone up by the amount of fake currency you printed. This is the same situation we analyzed when a government prints currency. Printing currency doesn't create money; it only steals it from others who trust the currency.

If printing currency doesn't work, then let's just go take some money. We'll find someone who has money, and force them to give it to us, or take it when they're not looking. Working through the foundations of money, we could force Adam to give us  an apple, or grab it when he's looking the other way. That's theft, though, and theft is punished by the government. We could force Adam to grow us an apple, but that's also a taking by force, and punished by the government. We don't want Adam's apple though; we want his money. Once we have his money, then we can go buy cheese or whatever we want. Adam's money, however, is his right to receive services from others, and taking it by force is also theft, and theft is punished.

How about if we borrow it from someone? We trade our promise to do something later in exchange for money (a universal promise). As the examples in the discussion of government borrowing show, we've not really increased our personal money supply. We have different kinds of promises on our balance sheet – our individual promise owed, some universal promises on hand – but our total of promises balances out.

We're not doing very well so far in finding some way to get more money. How do you get a lot of money? If we rule out taking it by force or fraud, then the only other way to get a lot of money is for someone to give it to you voluntarily in a fairly negotiated trade. You have to supply something someone else wants more than they want the money they give you. This really covers every possible way to get money. Let's look at some.

Let's start with an obvious one: you hire yourself out to dig holes for someone. They pay you money for each completed hole, and you dig a lot of holes. You now have a lot of money.

A little less obvious route: you build something, maybe a particular thing, or maybe a team of individuals with complementary expertise and interconnected relationships (a company). Someone gives you money in exchange for you allowing them to take the particular thing, or for you transferring your rights to the team's output. You now have a lot of money.

Some more subtle ones: you inherit it, or receive it as a gift. The original holder of the money thought the world would be more in line with their desires if you had the money. Maybe it was your rich uncle, or a secret admirer. It doesn't really matter why they thought that, they just did, and now you have a lot of money. You supplied something they wanted by being part of the world as they desired it. Nice work if you can get it, but you used no fraud or force so you're still ok.

Maybe you can find a really valuable thing. You discover a diamond in the dirt in your yard, or your horse gives birth to a really fast colt. If you have a right to the diamond, or the fast horse, then someone can give you a lot of money in exchange for transferring your rights to them.

What if you got your money by "exploiting your workers?" Does that count as voluntary? Remember our assumption – if the transaction was not voluntary, then you took it by force or fraud and the original acquisition was wrongful. But if the transaction was voluntary, then each party agreed that it was a fair deal. We may not like the difference in bargaining power, or a large difference in wealth, but our discomfort with the result is not reason enough for us to take away the freedom of the worker and the employer to make their own deal. If they are each free to make their own deal, then we have a wealth-improving voluntary transaction in money. If they are not each free to make their own deal, then we have force or fraud.

So, in all cases except force or fraud, the only way to get money is by giving something that is valuable to someone else, who freely gave the money in return. This is easy to see in digging holes, but is it true for inheritance and lotteries? If your rich uncle decides that he would prefer the world with you having a lot of money, then whatever you did as a nephew, even if no more than being alive, was worth the trade to your uncle. No one else might understand or agree with the choice, but we often don't agree with other people's choices as to how to spend their money. The fact that it was a gift, and involved a lot of money, doesn't change the principles.

But what did you do for others when you won the lottery? For a lottery to work, a large number of people must each spend a small amount of money for an even smaller chance of winning. When you bought your lottery ticket, you were giving the rest of the players a chance to play the lottery, a chance to win a big prize and the certainty of the thrill of the game. That was your contribution that justified the money you won. The jackpot is disproportionate to your expense, but the risk of that disproportionate outcome is part of the game (indeed, it's the key to the game).

OK, so the principles are easy to understand. Now, how do you actually get more money? The answer is in the foundations, and applies to an individual as well as to a society, but there are no shortcuts. Money is a promise to pay later for value provided now. **So, to get more money, you have to provide more value**. There are many ways to provide more value. You can work more hours, so that your total value provided is greater. This is limited by the number of hours in the day, however.

You can also provide more value in the same number of hours. Individually, this means tailoring your output to the desires of those with money – you produce today what is wanted by those who produced yesterday (that's why they have money today). This can be education, though only if Dr. You produces what is valued by others. A string of college degrees does not entitle you to more money; money is not a trade for who you **are** but rather for what you **do**. This can also be done by investment in tools. Someone with a tractor can dig more holes than someone working with a spoon. Again, having the tools doesn't get you money; more money comes from using the tools to produce more of an output valued by those who produced in the past.

In our complex and interconnected economy, many improvements in output are subtle and are often tied to small subsets of the people. Producing or finding rare things doesn't create money, unless other people want them. Even a small number of people, even just one, that wants your output gives you the ability to acquire money. There is no way around the foundation, though – if you want money, you have to produce something that someone else values.

These principles apply on a whole society level, as well. If a society desires to have more money, the temptation is to just print more currency, which just making more promises to themselves. Each new unit of currency, if it is to be money, represents a promise to provide some value in the future. Printing currency to pretend to have more money is the ultimate procrastination – we will not do anything more today, but we will enshrine in currency our promise to do more later.

As we've seen, printing more currency doesn't make more money, even when the whole society is behind the printing decision. Each unit of real money has to be obtained in trade for a value provided, in exchange for transforming the world to be more like the buyer wants it to be. A society's desire for more money is thus really a desire for more wealth. Absent force (conquering some other society) or fraud (stealing from some other society), the only way a society can acquire more wealth is to develop it. The people can work more hours, or be more productive, or acquire better tools, or desire things that are easier to acquire. In practice, people do some combination of all of those. Those societies that do not do any of those, do not become more wealthy. Those societies that erect barriers to those, by corruption or unchecked crime, reduce their ability to grow wealth.

To keep in mind:
1. **Money belongs to those who've produced value in the past.**
2. **To get more money, you have to produce something that those people value today.**
3. **This truth applies to individuals and to societies.**

IS IT GOOD FOR RICH PEOPLE TO HAVE SO MUCH MONEY?

It is popular in some circles to complain about rich people. From noted moralists to populist protesters, it is common to complain about the rich. They have too much money. They should give their money away to the poor. We should take their money from them. It's not right for one person to be so rich. At some point you've made enough money. We all do better when we spread it around.

Like all statements, these depend entirely on what the words in the statement mean. The only way to really understand what is going on is to start from the first principles and work our way up.

Let's deal with some easy ones first. If the rich person got their money wrongfully, then the complaint is not against how much money they have but rather against how they got it. The government can and should punish stealing $10 and can and should punish stealing $1,000,000. Getting money by force or by fraud is theft, and should be punished. As Theodore Roosevelt put it, "No man should receive a dollar unless that dollar has been fairly earned." The rest of this section will assume that the money was obtained through voluntary, above-board actions, and that we are truly looking at how much money someone has and not accusing them of stealing it. We are therefore talking about rich people who got a lot of money by creating a lot of value that their neighbors were willing to give money to acquire.

With that in mind, we don't have to be distracted about whether it was right for someone to get a lot of money. If acquired by force or fraud, we agree it should be punished. Acquired any other way, it was a voluntary transaction that the two parties involved agreed was better for each of them. But, even if there was nothing wrong or bad about how someone got money, we can still ask whether it is right or good for one person to have lots more money than his neighbors.

There are two ways for someone to "have a lot of money," and we need to look at them separately. Someone can have a lot of dollar bills in a room (or balances in bank accounts), or someone can own a lot of things that are translatable into money (for example, real estate or company stock).

The Money Room

Let's look at the money room situation first. Richie Rich of comic book fame, and Uncle Scrooge McDuck in the cartoons, both had rooms of money in their houses. They could just go look at it, or swim in it. While it may seem counterintuitive, that kind of rich person is actually temporarily impoverished, and the rest of society should be happy that they have all that money in the money room.

It seems strange to conclude that someone with so much money that they need a special room for it all would be impoverished, or that the rest of society is wealthier because of it. But let's go back to the principles, and look at what has really happened.

Each dollar that the rich guy has was obtained by a free trade of something of value for the dollar. The rich guy has given other people things or services they wanted, and received money in return. But remember what money is – the promise of a future service. So the rich guy has worked for his neighbors, and all he has taken in return is a bunch of IOUs.

Let's build on our previous examples to illustrate what is happening, by letting Adam get rich from his apples. Adam grows a lot of apples, and trades them to people. Adam doesn't take peaches or cheese in trade; in fact, all Adam takes for his apples is money. Adam spends a little of that money to live, and stores all the rest in his money room.

The question is whether Adam's money hoarding makes his neighbors better off, or worse off. How has the town changed by Adam storing that money? Everyone who traded with Adam got the apple they wanted, and gave up only a promise for something in the future. Until Adam spends money out of his money room, every apple receiver has effectively received an apple for free. Moreover, even if Adam does eventually spend money from his room, they have enjoyed the use of the apple for all the time that money was sitting in the room. They have also had the use of the peaches or cheese that Adam wants in return during all the time that money sits in the room.

So Adam's money hoarding makes everyone wealthier, except Adam. How can this be? Adam has all that money; how can he not be the wealthier one? The key to understanding this is to remember what money is. Money is just an intermediate form, used to translate people's promises across time. Money is not wealth. It is just something that you can trade for wealth. So Adam has a room full of potential wealth, while everyone else has the real wealth.

People who take money in trade have a loss of wealth while they hold the money. People with rooms of cash are losers, from a real wealth perspective. Being wealthy means that you have to spend money, not have money. Of course you have to have money to be able to spend it, but the increase in wealth comes from **spending** money, not from **having** money. As Benjamin Franklin put it: "Money never made a man happy yet, nor will it. The more a man has, the more he wants. Instead of filling a vacuum, it makes one." So the rich person who has all his money in a room is not a problem for society. In fact, he's a boon, providing value for his neighbors while only taking IOUs in return.

Even if it's ok for Adam to have his room of money, would be better if we spread the cash around? We could take the money out of Adam's money room and give it to other people. What have we done? Adam produced something of value, and traded it to someone for money, a promise to be given something of value at a later date. Now we want to go in and take those promises away by force. "By force" because if Adam will voluntarily give the money away (buying stale candy bars from his nephews, perhaps) then we are back into our former reasoning about voluntary trades using money.

But if we take Adam's money out of his money room by force, we are stealing. Adam trusted society in general to honor the promises that the money represented, and now society in general is taking those promises back. What do you think that will do to Adam's trust of society's promises in the future? To the trust of others who could produce lots of value? What would it do to yours? If you worked for someone, and they gave you money and then took it back? Would you keep working for them? Taking money by force from Adam starts to destroy the trust that is essential to money, at first just Adam's trust but also the trust of everyone who sees what happened to Adam.

But what about the people who received the money we took from Adam? Surely now they can spend the money, and everyone will be better off – you said that voluntary transactions always make everyone better off. Before answering this point, note that we are still stealing from Adam. However much we enriched others was exactly matched by what we stole from

Adam, and, if this theft is ok then all theft is ok (assuming that the robber being happier after the theft justifies the theft).

But let's use our foundations to examine what really happens. Wally gets some of Adam's money, and uses it to buy a tomato from Tom. This is like the Kenya money mystery at the beginning – the tomato existed without Adam's money, and Wally and Tom could have traded for a tomato at any time. Why did they need money from someone outside their transaction?

They needed Adam's money because Wally is like Questionable Quincy in our earlier example. Tom didn't trust Wally's promise to provide value later in trade for the tomato now, so Tom wanted Wally to produce some universal promise (money) to justify giving up the tomato. Wally didn't produce any value to get money on his own, so we gave him some of Adam's. So Wally's promise is backed up by Adam's productivity. But we just gave Adam a big incentive to not be so productive any more. We've taken Adam's productivity out of the picture, but left the currency in. When the government prints currency, there is more currency for each real promise (since the amount of currency is increased while the real promises are unchanged). When we take Adam's money by force, and penalize his productivity, we get the same effect –there is more currency for each real promise (since we've reduced the amount of real promises while leaving the amount of current unchanged). ,

If this seems hard to follow, consider the end points of the situation. Let's start with Adam owning all the money in the society, so he has all the available currency locked in his money room. What does everyone else do? Does everyone else starve until Adam decides to dole out some money? Of course not. People can still provide value, and make trades. Whatever they use to represent their promises for future value in trades becomes the new currency. Adam holding all the currency makes money inconvenient until a new currency is trusted, but Adam's currency doesn't do anything to the fundamental of money.

This is the key to the Kenya road money mystery. After some thought about the question, our host guessed that the Chinese money was needed because, if Kenyans tried to build the road, there would be too many people with "hands out" – wanting to get paid to let the road cross a particular piece of land, or to give permission for a group of workers to work, or to get to the job, or any number of requirements for such a project. The project needed someone else to start the trust, then each group could trust the others. The Chinese money enabled the project by enabling the trust, even though the Chinese money itself didn't buy anything that wasn't already owned by the local community. The Kenyans did not trust each other enough, in the form of money, to start the projects. They did trust the Chinese money, though, and the Chinese money started the chain of voluntary trades that built the road.

The net result of all this is that taking (by force or threats) money from someone who acquired it by voluntary trades hurts everyone in the long run. It is akin to inflation, since the promises and production that make money are separated from the currency that represents money. It also distorts money, since people can't trust that the universal promise that money must represent will be honored. If people can't trust that promise, then money is dying, and everyone's economic life is about to get much more difficult. Even worse, the people who have the most reason to stop trusting that promise are the people who've provided the most value for others, so we start killing our tree by cutting off the most fruitful branches first.

The Money Empire

The second situation where we talk about someone having a lot of money is when they don't have a lot of money in a room, but rather they have obtained a lot of money and traded it for other things. If the other things are consumables – peaches and cheese, or fancy vacations, or expensive toys – then they are just collecting on the promises made earlier. Adam grows one million apples, sells them and buys one million peaches. I don't think we can say anything negative about the impact on his neighbors from Adam satisfying his rather large desire for peaches by using his equally large ability to grow apples – we've just traded apples and peaches according to the desires of the individuals involved.

What if Adam buys productive assets, though, instead of consumables? Maybe Adam sells one million apples, and buys one thousand more acres of orchard. Maybe he buys stock in other companies that make stuff that people want. We would total up Adam's acres, and stock, and figure out what they would convert to in money, and say that Adam has a lot of money. If he kept all the money in a money room, we know everyone else would be better off. We also know that forcibly taking his money and spreading it around would be bad for society. But does Adam holding his money in land or companies help or hurt his neighbors? Is it better for all of us if we force him to give up some of his land or his companies? Even if spreading cash around is bad, maybe spreading productive assets around could still be good.

What about the land and companies, though? Those stay productive regardless of whether Adam owns them. Should we spread the ownership of land and companies around? Should we take them from the people who own them and give them to others? If we're not just stealing to enrich ourselves, then presumably we are going to spread them to everybody. Is that a good idea?

As always, let's look at the principles first. How did the owner get the money to buy more land or companies than the average person? He must have been better than the average person at supplying things that other people wanted. A lot of people traded money for something he supplied. So a lot of people have already voted (by spending money) that this person is good at figuring out and supplying what they want. Even if the money came by gift or inheritance, a lot of people voted (with their money) that the rich uncle was good at figuring out what people wanted. He may have made a poor decision deciding to give it all to the nephew, but the people already voted their confidence in his decision-making when they traded their money for whatever he supplied. Importantly, they voted not with paper ballots, or "likes" on social media, but with their actual money (meaning, they gave their own promises of future work in support of the uncle as good at supplying what they want).

If we are to take the productive assets, land or companies, from the guy who bought them, to whom shall we give them? Taking a single tractor and cutting it into millions of pieces is pretty obviously a wealth-reducing step. Taking an apple orchard and dividing it into a million little plots is also silly – how many apples can you grow on your twig? So we have to decide on someone to at least manage, if not own, the thing if we do not want to destroy its value.

How are we to decide such an important question, though? The world is too complex for everyone to know everything about everything, so we need to be sure the opinions of those who are closest to the action count the most. There are too many assets and too many people to hope to have any person or group make the decisions, so we need a system that can continuously self-identify those people. We also need to be sure we test the intensity and sincerity of each voter. We want this to also be self-regulating, so we don't have to test every person's statements about how much they care. Possibly the hardest part, we have to be able to conduct these votes continuously, about everything we have. People change, circumstances change; we have to be able to continuously vote and revote.

Bad news: there is no way to hold such a vote. Good news: we already have a way to hold such votes, and we already do it every minute of every day. Each person votes for the person best able to satisfy their needs when they spend money to buy the output. The people closest to the action automatically have the most say – diners in Dallas vote on restaurants in Dallas, and don't have much say about restaurants in Seattle unless they care enough to travel to Seattle. The intensity of each voter is already tested – one person can eat at the same restaurant every day if they really like it, or maybe once a month if it's pretty good but not really their favorite. The market conducts these votes continuously, about everything. Each person individually votes about everything around them by how they spend their time and money. Each person has the same amount of time. They have different amounts of money because they have made different uses of their time in the past, and their neighbors have rewarded their uses differently based on how much value their neighbors found in the output.

The continuous mess of shifting money and shifting ownership may never have it exactly right, but it constantly adjusts in pursuit of the right mix. It chases the optimal mix of incalculable variables as fast as possible from the aggregate decisions of everyone. It is never optimal at any given moment, but it is not possible for us to do better. The collected wisdom of all the people in the world participating in voluntary trades is the greatest parallel processing system imaginable for optimizing the allocation of resources.

Steve Jobs controlled a large company because he had proven over time that he was very good at producing things that people want. There was a time, however, when Apple was not as successful. People voted for other things instead of the Apple Lisa and the Apple Newton, so Steve Jobs had fewer resources to control since Apple was smaller. When Apple started producing and selling iPhones and iPads, people started voting for Steve Jobs again and he got more resources to control. The massively parallel decision making of the network of voluntary transactions relentlessly pushes resources toward those who make the best use of them as measured by everyone's aggregate satisfaction with the output. It is equally relentless in moving resources away from those do not – Polaroid's camera business is gone because people desired digital cameras more than they desired Polaroid's film cameras.

"None of us is as smart as all of us" is an occasionally popular saying. No one person, no defined group of people, no computer system, will ever be able to access all the information, weigh all the variables, make all the individual decisions, and take action on all that. The massively parallel, self-correcting system that is the free market is unbeatable.

To keep in mind:
It is not only right to allow people to keep money or wealth that they have acquired in voluntary transactions, it is also the best possible way to allocate resources for the good of everyone, as measured and expressed by everyone in their daily decisions about everything they buy (or do not buy).

WHAT CAN YOU DO IF YOU STILL THINK IT'S WRONG FOR SOME TO BE RICH?

You've gone through all the hard thinking about the foundation of money, and you understand how wealth is created and why someone having lots of it is ok. But you still think there is something wrong about some people being so rich while other people are so poor. What do you do about it?

Really, what you **do** about it is up to you. I want to help you understand how to **think** about it, so that whatever you do about it has some chance of working. So first, let's think about why you might object to someone being rich. It might be pure envy – you just want more stuff than you have, and you can't stand that someone else has more stuff than you do. Your options are pretty straightforward. You can take their stuff by force or fraud, and suffer the punishment that the government ought to dispense for takings by force or fraud. You can decide that you will produce more stuff, maybe even stuff that your least favorite rich person wants, so they will voluntarily give you some of their riches. This does good for you and them. Your last option is to leave things as they are, and just be miserable in your envy. This does no good for you, but at least doesn't do harm to anyone else.

People are not usually prone to confessing to pure envy as a motive, so, even when that is the motive, we usually have to understand more altruistic explanations. Whatever the motives, you have the same three options as before: take their stuff by force or fraud, produce something they will trade with you, or get used to disappointment. I know that's not very satisfying, since there is something that still seems not right about such disparities in wealth. There are some paths to the outcome you desire, though, if you use the tools you have developed in this reading.

Let's think a little broader about the situation. Someone has lots of money, and you don't think they should have so much. How do you change that? You can try to convince them to part with some of their money voluntarily, and enlist others to help you convince them. No force or threats or even trade of value needs to be involved. This works better than many realize. In 2011, almost $300 billion was given to private charities in the U.S. Most religions teach, and most people believe, that individuals have some moral obligation to help those less well off. Making the rich (meaning in this case, anyone who has enough to share) aware of a need, and reminding them of their moral obligation to help, can accomplish much. Like the nephew with his candy bar, you can try to convince the rich person that they value a world with better educated neighbors more than they value the amount of money you want them to contribute to your "educate the poor" initiative.

But we've all seen, or at least heard stories about, greedy rich folks who'd rather burn their money than give it someone else. While that's a popular stereotype, I don't know anyone like that, and I think such people are a lot less common than the media like to portray. I guess movies about decent people who work hard and share with others don't sell many tickets. But let's assume that you've found a greedy rich person, and want to do something about it. What legal and moral avenues are open to you?

First you can look at how they got their money, or are continuing to get their money. In concluding that some people having lots of money was not bad for others, we assumed that the rich people got their money without force or fraud. In the real world, this assumption might not be true. A rich armed robber got his money by force, and the government should punish him (including giving his money back to those from whom he stole it). A con artist who induces people to part with their money by fraud is in a similar situation.

Look closely at your rich person, and see if there is any force or fraud in how they conduct their business. Be careful, though, that you don't delude yourself. Being exceptionally good at something is not force or fraud - winning sports competitions or singing in front of large crowds or managing a high performing company are all legitimate ways of making lots of money (meaning, supplying lots of value that is traded voluntarily with others). Being smart or fast or strong, or having parents that gave you a stable home life and good education, or knowing people that can help you in your career, can all give you a tremendous boost in your earning capacity, but they do not signify force or fraud. Skill or luck in predicting what people will want is also not force or fraud – buying low and selling high, whether in stocks or collectibles or real estate, are also legitimate ways of making money. But if someone forces others to sell low, or lies about what they are selling high, then you may have a force or fraud complaint.

One of the most common ways that people get money by force or fraud is to hide their use of force behind the government's privilege to use force (sometimes called "crony capitalism"). A company produces a product that people will not buy at a profitable price, so the company lobbies the government to force the purchase. This can be direct, for example, by passing a law that everyone must have a certain safety product. This can be less direct, for example, by passing tax incentives that effectively force everyone to help pay for private party purchases of the product. It can be even more hidden when the government subsidizes certain businesses, forcing everyone to pay a share of a business's expense though their taxes.

If you find force or fraud in the business practices, whether direct or hidden behind government acts, then you have grounds to seek society's intervention. Force and fraud are bad acts, and someone who acquires money by force or fraud can be punished.

Your other approach is to reevaluate your measure of wealth, and your allocation of your own resources. Suppose you can't find force or fraud, either because the rich person is clean, or they've just hidden their wrongdoing effectively. Even if the rich person is engaging in purely voluntary, wealth-maximizing transactions, the fact that you are disturbed by their riches suggests that maybe all is not as it seems.

Remember again the example of the candy bar fund raiser. You buy the candy bar from your nephew, not because the candy bar itself is really worth your money, but because the combination of the candy bar, your nephew's happiness, and the cause he represents are worth your money. You make a transaction based on more than the simple monetary values of the items. This is true of most transactions – you trade money for food because the food makes your life better (or at least longer), even though the food does not have monetary value after you eat it.

How does this work with the rich person, making lots of money in voluntary transactions, that you still don't like? As regards your personal money, you can choose to buy from another supplier. That supplier might cost more, or have inferior goods, but remember you are making the transaction based on your total measure of wealth. In this case, your total cost is the money you spend plus the dissatisfaction you have from the rich person making more money. If that total cost does not outweigh the benefit you get from the rich person's product, then don't buy from the rich person. Another product, at a higher price but giving more personal satisfaction, might be the better deal. Buy a Samsung phone instead of an Apple phone if you don't think Apple's shareholders should get any more of your money (or vice versa if think Samsung has enough money already).

If that is not enough to cover your dissatisfaction, then you can try to persuade others to recalculate their own private transactions. This is still a trade for you, even though no money changes hands – you provide your services in educating others about how to value their transactions, and if you are successful you get a reduction in your dissatisfaction with the rich person's riches. You've traded your time and services in exchange for convincing others to act such that the world better conforms to your ideal.

I hope this doesn't sound too naïve. It has actually been quite successful. There are numerous examples of this in action. The most obvious are organized boycotts, but there are more positive expressions of this idea. The fair trade coffee movement tries to persuade individual coffee buyers to buy coffee that was produced under conditions that the fair trade folks think are better for the growers. When enough individuals start to factor that into their buying choices, then the businesses factor that into the selling choices. Today fair trade coffee is available at thousands of stores in the U.S.

There is also a movement today to persuade people to buy locally grown food. It might be more expensive in terms of money, but the argument is that the total value is worth the added expense. The total value can include the food itself, various qualities of the food, support for local growers, less risk of supply disruption, or less money to far away corporate farms. The aggregate purchasing decisions of many buyers generated money for the rich far away food company; changed aggregate purchasing decisions can change that.

To keep in mind:
1. It's silly to object to riches just because they exist.
2. It is meaningful, and right, to root out force and fraud, and to consider the richness of the seller when you decide what to buy if the richness of the seller causes you dissatisfaction.

MASTERING MONEY

There are some important conclusions that we need to keep in mind if we are to put money back in its place as a very useful tool, but not allow it to be our master.

First we have to demystify money. Hopefully the previous pages have helped do that. Money is not a mysterious thing. It is not some separate power in the universe. It does not have a mind of its own. It does not even have an existence of its own. Money is just people doing good things for each other, and people's promises to do more good things in the future. Money just represents the trust that we have in each other to follow through on those promises.

The second follows from the first. We need to turn down our fascination with money, and our deference to those with money. We might be fascinated with those who produce lots of value for others, and listen more closely to those who've proven to be good at providing value (if that's how they got lots of money), but the money itself should not be the cause. Someone with money can't **make** us do something. We are free people, and we can decide how we want to interact and trade with other free people. That often includes money, represented by currency, but if our interactions with others are governed by, or even dominated by, money, then we are indeed poor.

An improper esteem for money also leads to too much worry about money in the world. Too many people lose peace, and sleep, over whether they have enough money. Remember what money is, and how you get it. Money just represents value you have provided to others, and haven't yet received your actual reward. So, don't focus on getting money. Focus on providing value to others, and on wisely spending the money you have. If you don't have enough money, then you've not provided as much value to others as you want them to provide to you. Either increase your value creation, or decrease your demands on other people. There is no other way, no matter how much you worry.

We also have a lot of disputes over money. People fight over who has money, and how much money someone should have. These stem from ignorance about money, and cause several levels of hurt to people. They hurt in the short term, as we take the focus off productive interactions and trades and wrongly place it on currency. They hurt even more in the long term, as they undercut the trust in the promises of others that is needed for money to function. When you lose trust in money, that means that you've lost trust in the promises of your society. As history shows, no society survives that.

This is actually the answer to the mystery of money's power. When someone presents currency to us, we feel forced to accept it. Why? If we don't accept the currency, then we are questioning our own faith in all the currency-denominated promises of all those around us. A society where you cannot trust anyone is a scary place, and so we are afraid to reject currency. Communities with more barter transactions are less in thrall to money. Small communities often have transactions based more on personal trust in the individual and less on trust in the currency in his hand, and consequently are less in thrall to money. Communities with little access to outside money can still thrive on what's been called a "gift economy," where members of the community give to each other's needs based on trust in everyone's participation. Outside money is only needed when dealing with outsiders. In contrast, every time we let money or currency be the only unit of trust, we place ourselves more at risk of domination by whoever controls the currency.

We also need to be much more vigilant about those who can abuse the trust that we allow to reside in money. Anyone in position to create or manipulate currency should be highly suspect, and watched closely. Government creation of currency, and government-enforced fractional reserve banking, steal from us in ways that can be hard to see. Inflation, or the creation of currency not backed by value, has taken more wealth from people than any private thief ever could. It is a constant threat, and our energy fighting over money should be put into protecting the fundamentals of money. Otherwise, while we are fighting over a few eggs, the fox will be stealing the chickens.

While we are fighting over a few eggs, the fox is stealing the chickens.

Made in the USA
Middletown, DE
13 July 2016